NURTURING
THE
NURTURERS;
HEALING
THE
PLANET

lots of love & good
wishes dear Tony and
Angela,

from Leon & Annie

NURTURING THE NURTURERS; HEALING THE PLANET

THE WATI KANYILPAI STORY

LEON PETCHKOVSKY

Rev. date: 09/26/2020

To order additional copies of this book, contact:
Xlibris
AU TFN: 1 800 844 927 (Toll Free inside Australia)
AU Local: 0283 108 187 (+61 2 8310 8187 from outside Australia)
www.Xlibris.com.au
Orders@Xlibris.com.au
802041

CONTENTS

ACKNOWLEDGEMENTS

If I were to name everyone who has helped me with this over my life, I would need another book to list them. Let me just send all my loving gratitude to all my dear family members, my indigenous friends and mentors, and my dear colleagues.

May all be well with you, and may your lives continue to be filled with the love and compassion you exert so beautifully.

FOREWORD
The Wati Kanyilpai Story

In decades of work in remote disadvantaged indigenous communities in Central Australia, I was mentored by senior *ngangkari* (traditional healers) who helped me encounter the Wati Kanyilpai Dreaming. This is about a *male* Dreamtime ancestor whose task is to nurture the nurturers, to look after those who look after people, animals, and the land. The Wati Kanyilpai Dreaming focuses on the role that men can take in the healing project, as does this book.

In the last two decades, massive research in the developmental neurosciences (our understanding of how the brain grows in the first three years of life) confirms the vital importance of good nurturance in this period of life. The negative consequences of nurturance failure are vast. They include a range of emotional and psychological problems like depression, anxiety, learning and attention problems, poor impulse control, and problems with relationships. Metabolism is also severely affected. The immune system is compromised, and a range of conditions like diabetes and cardiovascular disease become more widespread. Because proper development of the right hemisphere is especially compromised, effects are beneath the conscious awareness of the individual. But they exert a huge influence on feelings and behaviours.

At the collective level, we see high rates of educational retardation, violence, crime and imprisonment, substance abuse, physical illness, and relationships problems, including a poor capacity to nurture children. Thus these problems are passed on in transgenerational cascades of misery. And yet there is poor awareness at the organisational and political level.

Because of the awful history of dispossession and alienation that indigenous people and their culture have endured, the children we work with in those disadvantaged indigenous communities are particularly affected. But childhood trauma is a global problem, affecting all of us in various ways. If we could only begin to address it properly, there would be massive flow-on effects, starting with happier, more functional individuals, and extending at its furthest level to collective issues like managing the planet more responsibly.

My colleague Professor Judy Atkinson is an indigenous woman who is developing programmes of restoration and repair in indigenous communities. Her thinking is that, as these communities heal, the healing effects can then pass on to larger communities, indeed to the entire planet.

This book looks at the distress in remote indigenous communities, how advances in developmental neuroscience can inform our repair and healing processes, and how we can extend this to the world at large. It focuses especially on how men can participate in this process, both to heal themselves and to help heal the planet.

CHAPTER 1

Caring for the Carers, Caring for the Planet
The Watikanyilpai Men's Dreaming

This book is addressed to my fellow men. We need your help.

We live in difficult times: domestic violence, terrorism, gross exploitation by various governments and financial institutions, ecological destruction, global warming . . . the list goes on.

How can we ease and amend all this?

We can start by learning about the enormous advances that have been made in our scientific understanding of human development in the first three years of life and its implications for our ailing world.

We will learn that developmental neuroscience explains how failures of nurturance during this critical period have disastrous psychological and physical consequences not only for the individual but for society in general.

We will then look at ways in which we can remedy this. Starting with ourselves, we will look at various ways of developing better empathy and mindfulness skills, better ways of looking after ourselves more adequately, and thus become better carers for vulnerable others in the emotional and interpersonal realms. This capacity to nurture the nurturers, to look after all the beings who already look after other beings, is a vital task if we are to save this suffering planet.

The Wati Kanyilpai Dreaming Story

Twenty-five years ago, I was camping out with my Jungian analyst friend and colleague Dr Craig San Roque with our Aboriginal medicine man teachers at Yarrapalong, a sacred medicine site near Yuendumu, in a remote part Central Australia. The Milky Way sparkled across the crisp desert sky. Our teachers had taken us to Yarrapalong because it houses the rock hole from which the Medicine Snake began his epic Dreamtime journey to the west through Lake Mackay to Nyinmi in Western Australia. This Medicine Snake Dreaming, known as **Wana Tjukurpa**, is one of the most important Medicine Dreaming songlines in Australia.

We were being taught some of the elements of Western Desert Aboriginal medicine by two wonderful *ngangkari* (the Western Deserts dialect word for 'traditional healer'), who are now deceased (*kumantjai*). We'd been invited to do this on the basis of some dreams that we had shared with Andrew Spencer Tjapaltjarri, another traditional elder, and our principal mentor.

Psychoanalysis treats dreams as psychodynamic metaphor. The patterning in the dream tells us something about the patterning of the patient's mind. But as Jungian analysts, Craig and I take this somewhat further. We also discern a teleological aspect, a finger pointing not only to our individual purpose on this planet (which Jung called the process of 'individuation'), but sometimes extending to even larger collective dimensions, groups, tribes, nations. Both of us therefore resonated deeply with Australian Aboriginal traditional approaches to dreaming, including that larger transpersonal Dreaming (*Tjukurpa*, in Western Deserts languages) that provides a foundation for all Indigenous Australian mythology and ritual.

We slept out under the stars, and Leon dreamt of a huge man, a loving ancestral being whose job it was to wander about from place to place, taking care of things by nurturing the nurturers, the young human and animal mothers, the plants, and the land. His tender nurturance extended across the entire planet, and he was especially focused on nurturing nursing mothers.

We shared this dream with our teachers, and they told us the name for this being was *Wati Kanyilpai*, the male being or man (*wati*) who continually looks after/nurtures everything (*kanyilpai*).

They told us that *Wana*, the Medicine Snake, helps medicine men (*ngangkari*) heal patients by taking on the patients' suffering. Wana had also seen how badly early nurturance neglect was affecting people, and therefore carried their pain as well. But he taught Wati Kanyilpai how to nurture the nurturers, and entrusted him with this global task so that future suffering could be prevented.

Many years later, as I look back at that experience and the planet and try to make sense of it as well as my own life's purpose, it seems clear to me that the most central issue for our planet at this time is for us to recognise the importance of how we care for other beings, how we take on Wati Kanyilpai's example.

The last two decades have seen an explosion in developmental neuroscience, informing our understanding of the importance of good enough nurturance in those first three years of life. When early caring goes wrong, networks in the brain which manage attention, impulse control, empathy, and mindfulness/

self-awareness become impaired and we slide inexorably into personal and collective/global disaster. If we can get that caring right at the very beginning, in those vital first few years of life, then a generation of more mindful, more empathic more caring human beings may treat each other, as well as animals and plants and the environment with some love and kindness.

Throughout this book, I will be channelling Wati Kanyilpai's loving intentions to you.

Nurturance is an awkward word but seems to be the only word we have in the English language to refer to the supportive, caring, and compassionately responsive processes that we bring to rearing our young, and also to how we interact more generally with other beings. Mythologically speaking, these concepts have traditionally been the responsibility of a range of earth and mother goddesses. But somewhat surprisingly, Wati Kanyilpai is a *male*.

We all begin our lives within our mother's uterus; she then gives birth to us and suckles us. Males cannot do this. But Wati Kanyilpai reminds us that men have a central role in supporting, protecting, and caring for those primary nurturers.

Wati Kanyilpai

To do this effectively requires a range of relational capacities that males need to develop further, if we are to nurture the nurturers in better ways. The women on this planet already have their arms full.

Be Me

I'm a foetus, six months old. My mother, Betty Napaljari, lives in a remote community in Central Australia. Betty herself has had a difficult beginning, with lots of stress and abuse, which is why she drinks a lot of alcohol and why I have the beginnings of foetal alcohol syndrome. Betty has no helpers because over the last hundred years, deculturation has made severe impacts on the traditional helper system. In the old days, she would have been looked after by a lot of culturally assigned helpers, sisters, and grandmothers. They would also have cared for me once I was born so that if Betty was sick or needed some respite, these women, who had already spent time with me developing some bonding, would have given her respite. But her culture is too fragmented for that to happen easily now.

My father Terry, her husband, also comes from a dysfunctional background, and has problems controlling his impulses. Terry often gets violent and threatens Betty. This frightens both of us. But there are many people like Terry in the community, and they too make for a very stressful larger environment for my mum.

*It will be another three months before I am born, but already, my amygdala, the brain centre that detect stress, are starting to come on line. As I sit in mum's womb, I can now begin to pick up **her** stress, as this inflames my amygdala. In turn, this affects my developing stress hormones and sets me up for a range of problems such as proneness to so-called metabolic syndrome, which includes obesity and diabetes. I tremble in Betty's womb.*

But things will get worse. When I am born, Betty will be too distressed to care for me properly. She will struggle to empathise or tune into me and this will reduce her ability to look after me. This will inflame my amygdala further and disturb my attachment to her. I will find it hard to control my misery, my moods, my capacity for paying attention to her and the environment, and my anger impulses. As I get older, I will have problems with forming good relationships with others, including any partners or children I may have when I grow up.

> *I am actually an intelligent baby, as you can see from my writing. But I will never reach my potential if she and I do not get intensive help.*
>
> *If we don't get such support, then when I grow up, I will struggle to be an effective parent. Any relationships I have with a partner will be painful and choleric. I will also get into trouble with the law. I will find it hard to get employment; I will be prone to a wide range of psychiatric and metabolic illnesses. Oh, and on top of all this, I will have a reduced life expectancy.*
>
> *Will someone* **please** *help me?*

Working to Heal Our Planet: The Core Arguments of Our Book

Why am I writing this? Why do I want you to read this?

We are living in interesting times—so much opportunity for good and for ill.

As a psychotherapist and a brain imaging neuroscientist, I know that the brain networks that serve empathy, compassion, and mindfulness develop well if the early caring we receive in those vital first three years of life is good enough.

This does not have to be perfect. But if nurturance is poor (abuse, neglect, high stress, gross mismatching) the stage is then set for a lifetime of misery.

Most of my patients come from this kind of early background, suffering from what is known as developmental trauma disorder. And this tends to get passed on to each successive generation unless we can intervene.

The problem is a global one, much larger than the limits of a psychotherapy session or the misery I see in disadvantaged indigenous communities.

The nurturance of our planet depends on how we nurture our nurturers. This is a time when men need to develop their nurturance role beyond the traditional one of hunter–gatherer, breadwinner, and defender against predators and enemies. In Chapter 3, I will be examining how recent advances in developmental neuroscience and attachment dynamics are highlighting the importance of a range of preverbal, intuitive empathy, and resonance skills that the females of our species employ naturally with babies. And in the final chapter, I will be offering recommendations on how we men can develop and enhance these abilities.

In the first three years of life, the right hemisphere of our brain develops a range of preverbal networks and functions which allow us to experience our relationship to ourselves, to others, and to the world in general. They occur preverbally, thus we have little awareness of them, yet they strongly influence our behaviours. The extent to which we are able to develop these functional networks depends upon the quality of nurturance we ourselves receive. Various forms of abuse, neglect, and mother–child synchrony malfunctions can generate a huge range of psychological and physical problems for the individual. There is also a transgenerational cascade effect.

Consequences for the broader society are also of great concern.

Failures of mindfulness (self-awareness) and empathy (awareness of the other) lead to increased violence and societal irresponsibility (warfare, terrorism, environmental and social exploitation—the huge dangers facing this planet). We need to act soon; there is little time left.

Nurturing the nurturers is the most effective way we can help, but there exists an enormous amount of societal and political neglect as well as denial around this issue. Men need to play a better role here, as Wati Kanyilpai reminds us.

This book overviews these matters and develops the scientific and sociological evidence. It also makes some recommendations (addressed mainly for my gender compatriots, the men on this planet).

Men and Nurturance

A good start in life for each new generation is the single most important determinant of how everything else will get nurtured—other people, animals, ecosystems, the planet.

Women have been providing this caring for their infants since the dawn of time. And yet, as I've said before, we still haven't even got a decent word for the process. The closest I can come to it is with the term *nurturance*, a term that sets many women's teeth on edge. The word for this in Western Deserts languages is *kanyintja*. There is a huge price that women (and their children) pay in patriarchal societies. The very qualities that allow men to provide some physical safety (hunting, fighting off bears and other intruders) can spill over onto how they treat the women. Thus a woman's life in such a society can be fearful, and this spills over into the infant's developing brain and, in turn, into the larger society as a transgenerational cascade.

Hilary Clinton recognised this many years ago. Her Hilary Doctrine is developed in the culminating chapter of *Hard Choices*, a memoir of her time as secretary:

> It was no coincidence that the places where women's lives were most undervalued largely lined up with the parts of the world most plagued by instability, conflict, extremism, and poverty. This was a point lost on many of the men working across Washington's foreign policy establishment, but over the years I came to view it as one of the most compelling arguments for why standing up for women and girls

was not just the right thing to do but also smart and strategic . . . the correlation was undeniable, and a growing body of research showed that improving conditions for women helped resolve conflicts and stabilize societies. 'Women's issues' had long been relegated to the margins of U.S. foreign policy and international diplomacy, considered at best a nice thing to work on but hardly a necessity. I became convinced that, in fact, this was a cause that cut to the heart of our national security. (Clinton 2014, *Hard Choices*, p. 562)

In *any* society, the expectations on women are overwhelming. The girls have to do all of the emotional nurturing. No wonder so many women feel fed up and exploited.

It is time that men began to develop more emotional nurturance. But who will nurture men to make them more nurturant? Women have enough on their plates, and we can't rely on angels or aliens to do the job. The responsibility falls back on us **men**.

As I reflect on this, I thank all the women in my life for having helped me develop whatever emotional intelligence, whatever nurturance skills I have. The core purpose of this book is to encourage my fellow males in this path. Without it, there is no long term hope for Planet Earth.

The Anthropocene on the Brink: Armageddon or the New Jerusalem?

Anthropocene is the term often used to refer to the geological epoch of human occupation on this planet. Life on this planet has never been easy, but our current era presents some unique challenges (and opportunities). The Anthropocene seems to me to be on the brink of transformation. We have weapons of mass destruction, global terrorism, and the widening gap between the mega-rich and the rest of us. There is also the threat of disastrous climate change and the devastation of ecosystems brought on by mindless exploiters and polluters. All of these horrors may well get worse and plague our grandchildren and the planet we inhabit if we don't do something about them. Even so, there is much resistance to the work of global healing. Some of this resistance lies within me and you, despite our very best intentions, perhaps in the form of a kind of numbed detachment brought on by reluctance to contemplate all of the pain and horror?

We have a hard enough time coping with our own suffering, let alone extending that to the pain of other beings, and this reluctance pervades our global social ecosystem. It is not just the generation of pollutants but a mentality that underlies it, informs societies, and the people within them. It is not just the CO_2 that needs to be reduced but the human systems that generate it which need to change. It is time for the next evolutionary leap in global human sentience. The choice is clear: leap forwards or face global disaster. We need to develop a critical mass of mindful and empathic people on this planet. This is not easy to do. We must also reduce the level of human dysfunction which makes this task so difficult.

We know now that we may actually have the means to reduce the level of behavioural and psychological disorder (mental illness, narcissism, psychopathy, violence and criminality, drug addiction) on this planet by at least some 20 per cent (Teicher 2003). With focused efforts, we could probably increase the proportion of human beings with well-developed empathy and mindfulness (awareness of self-process) by 10 per cent. Recent developmental neuroscience findings point that the core problem is neglect, abuse, and failures of attunement during the first few years of life. This is because it damages our capacity for empathy and mindfulness, and boosts a large range of behavioural psychological and physical dysfunctions that generate transgenerational cascades of distress. The strategy of repair is to find ways of effectively nurturing the nurturers.

Why is this so central? If we can begin to address the very beginnings of how our human capacity for empathy, mindfulness, and impulse control develops, we address the fundamental solutions to many human problems.

There is always huge resistance to such change. Some of it is simply the usual selfish and violent forces at work. But as we mentioned earlier, some of it is more subtle, because it can come from basically good and kind human beings. That is what we want to examined because it is at this level that changes are most likely to begin.

Wati Kanyilpai Would Like You to Try This Exercise

Wai, walytja tjuta (Greetings, dear fellow beings). *Niyanganiy* (have a good look)! Bring some mindfulness to what is arising in your thoughts sensations and emotions as you read this. Take note of any irritation or resistance (*pikarti*) you may be feeling at this moment.

Does it arise out of deeper feelings of despair, hopelessness, a mistrust of the science that supposedly underpins some of these fears? Throughout this book, I will be encouraging you to pause occasionally and take stock of what is going on inside you—a little mindfulness exercise.

Do that with me right now.

When I claim that we might just achieve, through nurturing the nurturance process, the critical mass of functional humans needed to save the planet from some of the ongoing destructive processes that threaten it, do you feel like scoffing? Just note it, and find some tenderness in your heart.

You, Me, and the Universe

It is true that you and I are all tiny wavelets in and of this vast and mysterious cosmic ocean. Our planet is a larger wavelet but still so relatively tiny. Everything is interconnected in time and space, a part of the vast ocean of buddha nature if you like. Consciousness is precious, and yet it struggles with its awareness of interconnectedness. We haven't yet connected with other interstellar forms of consciousness. And we struggle to connect lovingly with each other and other life forms on this planet. How can we develop a critical mass of empathic and mindful humans who could begin a radical transformation, an emergence of a caring new form of planetary culture per John Lennon's 'Imagine'?

This will depend largely on how well we nurture the nurturers on this planet over the next generation.

This Little Wavelet

I, the tiny speck writing this book, began his life as the baby of a woman who was the last child in a Russian family of twelve daughters. Valentina was fostered off at the age of seven. She grew up to be good, brave, and loving woman, but she was badly emotionally damaged. In *this* century, she would be diagnosed with developmental trauma disorder. Thus as a child, I put a lot of energy into mothering *her*. At the time it just seemed so natural to do. This explains my choice of occupation—why as I matured I was drawn to become a psychotherapist. I could then try to heal other deprived beings and maybe get some vicarious repair. It took me decades of psychotherapy, meditation, and mindfulness training to realise this and patch myself up to the point where I could be a good enough parent and therapist.

My patients have also mostly come from a background of early childhood neglect and abuse (as do the majority of *all* psychiatric patients). My contact with those dear people has combined more recently with my interests in functional brain imaging and the developmental neurosciences. My ability to become a better psychotherapist has been helped by the advances I see in this field, as I learn how vital the first three or four years of life are to our developing brain circuitry. This is especially so for the right hemispheric, limbic, and hindbrain pathways and programmes which sustain empathy (kindly awareness of the other), self-awareness/mindfulness, and vigilance settings (whether we habitually live in states either of chronic anxiety / depression / hyperarousal, or a certain degree of inner peace / equanimity).

After completing my studies in medicine and psychiatry, I trained as a Jungian psychoanalyst and began attending intensive meditation retreats. My personal psychoanalyses and meditation experiences, plus the work I do with patients, made me more aware of how early preverbal right hemispheric and limbic patterns manifest in the attachment dynamics and interactions in psychotherapy as well as in our wider interactions with the world around us. I have also taken an active research interest in functional brain imaging (fMRI and QEEG) and have published several studies in this field, contributing to the substantive developmental neuropsychobiology research literature that points to the centrality of early nurturance processes in facilitating the development of physical and psychological health and resilience. While doing this and considering the organisational and political dimensions (such as child services, mental health services, mental health policies), I became increasingly appalled at how ill-informed some of these interventions were in terms of the value of empathy and mindfulness in their practice and the central role of early nurturance in their philosophy. Some seemed actively antagonistic. Nurturance failures have serious consequences for individuals and society. Yet there seems to be little organisational or political awareness of this at the policy level.

How does that resonate with those of you working in various people-helping fields?

In my visits to remote and disadvantaged Aboriginal communities over more than three decades, I have observed how they suffer disproportionately and how the larger Australian community, seemingly poorly informed of the importance of early nurturance, has failed to provide adequate repair despite many interventionist programs. The consequences include reduced life expectancy; high violence, suicide, and imprisonment rates; and a range of illnesses (metabolic syndrome) associated with hypophyseal pituitary adrenal (HPA) axis damage resulting from high maternal and infantile stress. Foetal alcohol spectrum disorders, sensory processing disorders, attention deficit hyperactivity disorders, conduct disorders, and learning disorders are prevalent in this child population.

Developmentally traumatised mothers in those environments, in their effort to nurture their infants in an already stressful environment, can unwittingly hand down their own developmental trauma to their children, and it gets worse with each generation. In addition, epigenetic modifications (like the methylation of a range of genes associated with neurotransmitter expression) add a multiplicative genetic susceptibility component to this transgenerational cascade. And this will continue to get worse with each generation unless we begin to nurture the nurturers more helpfully. But all these processes apply equally strongly to the wider community, as we know well in the mental health domain, where the overwhelming majority of our patients have backgrounds of early developmental trauma and problematic early nurturance.

A Huge Dilemma

Although I have written many scientific and academic papers, I had consistently resisted the thought of writing any kind of book, feeling I would simply add yet more jabbering to the global writing glut. But the notion of finding some way to encourage the nurturing of the nurturers (caring for those stressed young mums in the pre- and perinatal period and the first three years of the babies' lives so that their babies can get an optimal start in life) and its potential for helping transform this suffering planet were just too compelling.

Writing about such a topic is not without its integral problems. One big problem is that championing a paradigm of 'nurturing the nurturers' will inevitably offend, however unintentionally, many mothers on this planet. They will likely feel criticized, marginalized, patronised.

Here is what happened when I ran the idea of a book on 'nurturing the nurturers' past Rachel, my eldest daughter.

Leon: I want to write a book on 'nurturing the nurturers'. The nurturing we receive in the first few years of life has a big influence on our mental and physical health. It shapes our own ability to be nurturers, our capacity for empathy in the way we relate to each other, other life forms, and our planet. Why does nurturance get so little air time?

Rachel: Oh, *Dad*, the word itself is so *gawky*. And what does it actually mean? But more important, every mum will think of a thousand times they did or felt or thought the wrong thing, another thousand times when they didn't have a clue. I was at a friend's house the other weekend and we as mums were talking the hard sides of mothering—those moments (sometimes extended) of loss of control. Nobody tells you that that is going to happen. Parenting books and theories make it sound as if all that can be simply ironed out. So there is always a background fear that 'I am not good enough' as a parent (friend, partner, person . . .), that my job will produce a little Hitler, or more simply someone who has trouble loving/respecting me (and themselves and others) when they grow up. Narcissistic! It's just so painful. As if we don't get blamed enough eh?

She then reminded me that as if this is not hard enough, there are the so-called mommy wars—the ongoing conflict between the 'working mum' and the 'stay-at-home mum' condition.

Where Are the Men?

I am very aware that many women might find the above painful, but what about men's reactions to nurturance? I suspect because so much nurturance is right-brained and preverbal, the average male with his left-brain preoccupations will struggle to come to grips with it and be either dismissive ('It's more important to ensure the economy is growing, the borders are protected . . . whatever') or tokenist (politicians kissing babies).

From earliest caveman times, male nurturance had to do with slaying predators, catching fish, and keeping the tribe safe from other human assailants. Today's equivalent is the breadwinner. The more bread he wins (Donald Trump), the more highly regarded he is as a nurturer. But what is missing is the emotional, relational component of nurturance.

But how is this going to be developed? There is so much resistance—often simply mindless refusal to consider the problem at every level: national, professional, educational, or early developmental. Thoughtful women often tell me that even they notice a subtle resistance to their husbands' engagement with the babies. And yet what is needed is precisely that men become better emotional relational nurturers in order to support the primary caregivers (usually women) of the babies. Where best might men learn this than from engaging with the babies in an environment which supports their efforts?

Kensho, a Moment of Awakening

How does all this work in our lives?

When Agnes started treatment with me in her early twenties, she had been a mess from the very beginning of her life. Her mother, Amelia, became badly depressed soon after giving birth and despite all her best intentions, struggled to look after her baby's emotional needs. The infant Agnes developed many of the emotional and behaviour problems we see in early nurturance dysfunction. (We will describe this at length in this book). But things got even worse. When Agnes was five, she developed leukaemia and spent a whole year in hospital for the various treatments. Agnes survived, but the stress and prolonged separations from her mother Amelia left her with deep psychological wounds. It took over three years of intensive therapy for her to begin to get better. Towards the end of this time, she actually found a supportive partner, Bernie, and got pregnant. Baby Louise was now three months old, and Grandmother Amelia brought her to see me at the end of one of Agnes's sessions.

Baby Louise and I gazed into each other's eyes. It was a long moment of mutual seeing, a melting away of any sense of self or separation, a meeting with Buddha or Jesus, what Zen calls *kensho*. In Japanese, *ken* means 'seeing', *shō* means 'essential nature'. Seeing is different from looking. When we *look*, we bring our agendas and 'brain glasses' into the process. When we *see*, we are simply there, unencumbered by preconceptions. Young babies have that clear, unclouded mind until it gets disabused by life's many impacts.

The women's faces began to glow with a blissful serenity. *Kensho* can be so contagious. In that moment, I thought, *Louise is going to get a good start in life. The transgenerational cascade of misery can actually be broken.*

My only regret was that Bernie had not been present to share this moment.

This book is, I hope, a tiny step in our Wati Kanyilpai project, helping men become better emotional nurturers of the women nurturers. For those of you men out there who are actually reading this thing, please persevere, because we will be discussing various ways in which male emotional nurturance can be enhanced and how it will actually be good for you *and* the planet. Some of you will actually have bought this book for yourselves. Take in our gratitude. Without you, this planet is doomed. For many more of you, a woman in your life will have given it to you as recommended reading. Take in her generous intentions. She wants to help you develop more empathy and mindfulness not just for her own sake and the sake of any children involved but also for your own well-being. She wants to nurture *you*.

> *Wati Kanyilpai says 'Dear men, just take a moment to reflect on your reactions to the word* nurturance *(*kanyintja*).'*

To All My Fellow Wavelets: Apologies and Invitations to Contribute

How can we begin to address these dilemmas? We can certainly start by making a huge pre-emptive apology to all the mums on this planet. The contents of this book are not meant to criticise, hurt, or offend you, but the topic is such a sensitive one that feelings will inevitably be bruised and stung. I apologise whole heartedly for any pain I cause, however unintended.

A part of this apology includes my commitment to foster my fellow males in developing our capacity to nurture the nurturers; the principal aim of this book; to contribute to a macro-culture that wants to nurture the nurturers, and includes expectancy of repair. So please feel free to comment and criticize. This is a necessary part of the ongoing dialogue this planet needs around the subject.

And the second thing I can do is to ask you all to contribute: how do you think we can we best help mums in a 'good enough' way in those critical early years? You could send me thoughts and ideas via my Politics of Nurturance blog, http://watikanyilpai.com/. There is also an online interactive version of this book to interact with.

There are also many organisations that are beginning to address this vital issue, and I encourage you all to bring your powers of persuasion to people who are involved in the various organisations that can and should be encouraging the delivery of nurturance. These include various child welfare and mental health services and various political organisations. What I would love to see is a global awareness, a global movement that values and prioritises early nurturance, with its potential to transform life on our aching planet.

This Larger Wavelet Called Planet Earth

There is the earth, its geology and ecosystems. But in this period, a critical part of the ecosystem is the human population and the various cultures it has created and its global impact.

We are on the cusp of transformation. As we said earlier, if we could somehow reduce the level of behavioural and psychological disorder (mental illness, violence and criminality, drug addiction) on this planet by 20 per cent (Teicher 2003) and if we could increase the proportion of human beings with well-developed empathy and mindfulness (awareness of self-process) by even 10 per cent, we might just achieve the critical mass needed to save the planet from some of the ongoing destructive processes that threaten it. Such a development may actually be possible.

This book aims to overview the neurodevelopmental neuroscience findings concerning how failures of nurturance contribute to those problems, and how these could be reduced. And it shall overview how good quality nurturance enhances empathy and mindfulness.

Excruciating Pain

Nurturance is a highly sensitive topic, and, as we have seen, talking about it can often cause even those who provide adequate nurturance to feel criticised. But this is much worse for damaged nurturers, women whose own infant background has been difficult, who were abused and neglected in various ways, and left with varying degrees of developmental trauma disorder (DTD), the term used by Bessel van der Kolk (van der Kolk 2014), one of the world's research leaders in this field. We will be expanding on the concept of DTD in the next chapter.

Unfortunately, DTD, as well as impairing one's capacity for providing good nurturing, often also drives one to have children, sometimes at an extremely young age. (Damaged impulse control? An intuitive drive to repair one's own damage vicariously through the children?)

DTD makes people exceptionally sensitive, and clumsy attempts to nurture them will be counterproductive. The helpers—individual case workers, managers of relevant help programmes, and the organisational cultures that support them—need to develop appropriate awarenesses and skills, a steep emotional learning curve. We shall address this in greater detail in this book. But for the moment, let us remember that mistakes can sometimes be golden opportunities. As child psychoanalyst Donald Winnicott reminds us, 'good enough' nurturance needs to be just that: good enough, not perfect. In fact, lapses are absolutely essential because they create an opportunity for repair, and once this has happened several times, a microculture is created that includes expectancy of repair This in turn makes for a much safer and more secure environment. It is no longer a case of 'one mistake and the sky falls down forever'.

Humans with awful early histories and oversensitised brain circuitries get their buttons pressed, often unwittingly, and lash out. On this planet, we put trillions of dollars into weapons of mass destruction, with the ostensible justification of providing some protection. How much more protection would we get if we put one hundredth of this money into effective measures to nurture the nurturers and protect the babies and infants?

More recently, a lot of people have begun writing on the role of empathy at a global level. Two authors in particular come to mind: Jeremy Rifkin in *The Empathic Civilization* (Rifkin 2010) and Roman Krznaric in his book *Empathy; a Handbook of Revolution; and Why It Matters, And How to Get It.* (Krznaric 2015). Their books are clearly steps in the right direction, yet alarmingly, awareness is missing even within their writing of the crucial importance of programs for fostering the nurturance process during those first years of life so that the next generation can bring more empathy into the world.

How to Mend All This, Especially from Men's Perspective?

In the next few chapters, we will look at the following:

- How contemporary developmental neuroscience and attachment studies have identified the first three years of life as the critical period in which the brain function and networks to do with empathy mindfulness and impulse control develop, for good or ill. Religions and politicians have yet to recognise this fully.

- How the obvious key response is to nurture the nurturers. *This is a vital men's task.*
- To do that, we have to identify the mums at risk, while avoiding stigma, and nurture them in ways that are sensitive enough for them to take in.
- But we need to develop high-level mindfulness and empathy skills to do this sensitively.
- This book therefore speaks to the *male* reader as if *you* are a vulnerable mum yourself. So unless you are actually pregnant or rearing an infant, you will *have* to use your empathy skills to put yourself in *their* shoes.
- Nurturing the nurturers extends beyond individual mums and includes nurturing the environment and encouraging organisations and political processes to recognise the centrality of the nurturance process and to support it.
- We shall visit Central Australia and see how transgenerational cascades of developmental trauma develop in disadvantaged indigenous communities.
- We will look at some case studies to illustrate positive interventions.
- We shall broaden the discussion to the larger non-indigenous sphere
- We will see how there is a lack of centralised awareness of early nurturance across *all* religions.
- This is also the case to an alarming degree across all political systems and nations. Even the Greens leave out

the early human nurturance dimension. Let's save the trees, but what about the babies?

- And we will finally look at ways to remedy this lack and make our contributions towards the next stage of planetary evolution, with a focus on what **men can do** as nurturers of nurturers.

You will have noticed by now that, at various times throughout this book, I invite you to slow down and check into what is going on in you—the sensations, feelings, thoughts, images, memories that come up at various moments—and to do that in a kindly but very open way, with an open mind and open heart, a moment of mindfulness. Wati Kanyilpai invites you to do this.

> *Kuwari palyani, munta uwa. Do that now, please. It does not matter whether what comes up is angry, critical, resigned, hopeful, sharp, inchoate, whatever. What matters is that you simply pick up what is going on for you at the moment, and stay with it in a kindly manner long enough to see what evolves, what happens next. That process is the heart of the matter. This is about what is going on in us and how we can use our awareness of the fluctuating nature of these processes so we can begin to change the world for the better.*

BIBLIOGRAPHY

Clinton, Hilary (2014). *Hard Choices*. Simon and Schuster.

Krznaric, R. (2015). *Empathy: A Handbook of Revolution* and *Empathy: Why It Matters And How To Get It*. Penguin Random House.

Rifkin, J. (2010). *The Empathic Civilization*. Penguin Press. ISBN 1-101-17042-5.

Teicher, M. H., Andersen, S. L., Polcari, A., Anderson, C. M., Navalta, C. P., Kim, D. M. (2003). 'The Neurobiological Consequences of Early Stress and Childhood Maltreatment'. *Neuroscience & Biobehavioral Reviews, 27* (1), 33–44.

Van der Kolk, B (2014). *The Body Keeps the Score*. Viking 2014: ISBN10 0670785938 ISBN13 9780670785933.

CHAPTER 2

The Global Perspective
Megamemes that Shape our World

My granddaughter Harlow and I were sitting in the garden one evening, smelling the roses. She turned to me and, seemingly out of nowhere, said, *'The world is sooooo huge—so many many people and animals and plants.'* Then she looked up into the sky at the Milky Way. *'And our world is so tiny, a speck among the million stars.'*

And I remembered, in that moment, that Wati Kanyilpai, who started his loving journey in Central Australia, did not confine his travels to Australia's shores but went out ***everywhere***, the whole world, the entire universe.

Wati Kanyilpai's World

Let us go with him now and look at the larger picture with compassionate eyes. Questions arise: what has been happening on this planet over the eons? What *could* happen?

What if there were critical masses of nurturing males on this planet who tended babies and the mothers of those babies, ensured that babies lived in environments free of domestic violence, and surrounded by supportive extended family and social networks? What if the men encouraged organisations both at the grassroots and at the national political level to value and prioritise good nurturance during those vital first thousand days of infant life? What if this culture used good early nurturance as the primary lens through which to evaluate every social policy and activity?

The impact at the global level of good or bad nurturance is the core theme of our conversation. It is important therefore to look at the wider sociocultural context within which contemporary advances in our understanding of developmental psychology emerge. This includes an understanding of causation and an overview of some of the major cultural factors that have been shaping global culture (the Anthropocene oven) in the last four hundred years or so.

Cause and Effect: Tricky Subjects

One basic issue underpinning all our discussions is the difficult subject of 'cause and effect'. We must be able to demonstrate a reliable causal linkage between quality of early nurturance and a range of good and bad outcomes in later life.

This issue also applies to how the products of good nurturance might have an impact in reductions in our global burden of ego-centeredness violence, crime, and psychological/relational dysfunction.

Let us begin by examining some of the most basic processes that underlie our understanding of these elements.

Cause and Effect and Those Vital Early Years of Life

Causality can be a deeply perplexing principle, because statistics are population-level notions that do not apply to individuals. For example, at the population level, poor availability of food leads to reduced health in the population, but at the individual level, there will be *some* people who will do well for a variety of reasons.

This problematic notion of causality is the situation we find ourselves in when we look at how early nurturance impacts on later human behaviour.

No one can predict with 100 per cent accuracy that even with the very best early start in life, any **one** particular individual will turn out well. But one **can** guarantee that a society that values early nurturance will turn out more healthy functional individuals than one that doesn't.

Genetic (1), environmental (2), and developmental (3) factors all play a part in how we develop from babies to adults. And they interact with each other. For instance, studies (Dadds et al 2012, Fallon 2013) suggest that a baby with a genetic predisposition for psychopathy may paradoxically develop into a **more than average** caring adult if engaged in eye contact (*kensho* moments?) and mindfulness and empathy therapies/practices at a developmentally receptive stage (probably before puberty).

We know that there are people who receive a good and caring early nurturance and yet still end up with psychopathy or schizophrenia, but they are a minority. And we also know there are some people who have an abusive or neglectful childhood and yet come through it as kind, resourceful human beings, though again these are in a minority, like the few lifelong smokers who evade cancer. But all our observations suggest that problematic nurturance loads the dice hugely towards negative outcomes at the collective level.

There are some large cultural-historic factors at work in our present world, shaping the human ecosystem. Let us look at them.

Five Memes That Inform the Anthropocene

The term *Anthropocene* refers, of course, to that period during which human activity has been the dominant influence on climate and the environment, perhaps the last twenty thousand years.

The term *meme* was first proposed by Richard Dawkins (Dawkins 1989) who wrote:

> *We need a name for the new replicator, a noun that conveys the idea of a unit of cultural transmission, or a unit of imitation. 'Mimeme' comes from a suitable Greek root, but I want a monosyllable that sounds a bit like 'gene'. I hope my classicist friends will forgive me if I abbreviate mimeme to meme. If it is any consolation, it could alternatively be thought of as being related to 'memory', or to the French word même. It should be pronounced to rhyme with 'cream'.*

It refers to an idea, a behaviour, or style that spreads from person to person within a culture. It acts as

> *a unit for carrying cultural ideas, symbols, or practices that can be transmitted from one mind to another through writing, speech, gestures, rituals, or other imitable phenomena with a mimicked theme. Supporters of the concept regard memes as cultural analogues to genes in that they self-replicate, mutate, and respond to selective pressures.* (Dawkins in Wikipedia)

There are memes and megamemes. As I look over the last five hundred years, there are several *major* cultural shapers that are so powerful that they can change not just organisations or nations but the entire Anthropocene.

The first and most obvious megameme is the ***scientific*** one that emerged in the European Renaissance. From then on, we no longer accepted things unconditionally because some supreme authority had stated that '*it must be so*', '*I have written it*', '*God has said so*', etc.

For ***the very first time*** on this planet, we no were no longer utterly subservient to authoritarian proclamations. We, like Galileo, put things to the test, and if they conformed to scientific scrutiny, they were considered to be worth relying on. If not, then they remained in the realm of supposition, theory, or hypothesis. As we all know now, the Roman Catholic Church of the time did not like Galileo's scientific observation–based assertion that the Earth moved around the Sun, and the church fought to retain the notion that the Earth was the centre of the universe. But ultimately, the scientific mindset prevailed, and it has continued to profoundly change our culture and our world. The first megameme we recognise here is that of ***scientific objectivity***.

There are, of course, domains that do not yield so readily to the classical scientific method. The so-called human sciences (like psychology) necessarily involve considerations of subjectivity, the felt and lived experience of every one of us, which cannot be analysed in the way that we can objectively examine a chemical compound, or literally pinned down and dissected like a laboratory rat. And here, the megameme that stands out in my mind is the one developed by Freud, with his 'free association' method for the treatment of patients as they lay on his couch. For ***the very first time ever*** on this planet, it was possible for one human being to say to another whatever was on their mind, however trivial, momentous, obscene, stupid, insulting, whatever, without fear of repercussions. Admittedly though, this was confined to the psychoanalytic treatment room.

In earlier times, such spontaneous comments could have very negative results: your head could get cut off, you could be sent to gaol, or you could be forced to recant or beg forgiveness. Freud's method now provided a radical new freedom. Though Freud confined this to the psychoanalytic couch and the psychoanalytic hour, the principle has gradually extended to a wide range of other domains and has surreptitiously contributed to free speech. We will call this second megameme '*freedom of expression*', and it is changing our planet, despite fiercest opposition.

A third megameme is the one of *global consciousness*. Media, the internet, and electronic communications have created— again, *for the first time* on this planet—the conditions that can enable all of us to communicate with each across the globe, despite the various efforts of powerful individuals and organisations to censor, limit, or frustrate this process for their own ends. However much some of us might disregard it, we are now all part of the global culture.

The fourth megameme that is being proposed here will strike many readers as very controversial. We mentioned it earlier in our discussion of causality. It is the central message of this book: a recognition of *the centrality of early nurturance in human development*. It comes as something of a shock to realise that although human beings have always had some intuitive sense of this, it was not clearly articulated until the child psychiatrist and psychoanalyst John Bowlby began to study the process and write about his findings. His interests were driven by his own childhood experiences of maternal neglect.

Bowlby's mother, like many other mothers of her social class, considered that parental attention and affection would lead to dangerous spoiling of the children. She thus would only see him for an hour each day. The rest of the time, he was looked after by his nanny Minnie, who, fortunately for Bowlby (and *us*), was so warm and nurturing that even though she had to leave the family before Bowlby turned four, she helped him lay down a sufficient enough good internal attachment dynamic and capacity for emotional regulation that he was capable of withstanding many further stressors and grow up to be the empathic and mindful being who recognised the damage that children living in hospitals and orphanages and experiencing war-time separation suffered from (maternal deprivation), and who developed the details of attachment theory (Bowlby and King 2004).

As this fourth megameme took hold, for *the first time ever* in the planet's history, we began to look in detail at and describe what happened in the first few years of life between mothers and their babies, and we began to acknowledge from a scientific perspective that bad nurturance led to massive problems, whereas good nurturance gave children an improved chance to develop their good potential into adulthood.

We might call this megameme the *developmental nurturance* meme. Its application at a global level may well make the difference between catastrophe and progress for this quivering planet. This is Wati Kanyilpai's loving mission.

We have thus far described four megamemes:

- *scientific objectivity*, which tells fact from fancy;
- *freedom of expression*, which allows us to openly articulate this and many other things;
- *global consciousness*, across the entire world;
- *developmental nurturance*, which increases the likelihood of more empathic and mindful human beings on this planet.

And the four megamemes are interactive. The *scientific* perspective interlocks with *freedom of expression*, the means to do this *globally* through electronic communication, and the capacity of *developmental nurturance* to influence all of these for the better.

Two of the megamemes are simply incontestable: the scientific revolution and global communication.

Freedom of expression is subtler Voltaire is quoted as saying, 'I disapprove of what you say, but I will defend to the death your right to say it.'

The notion of free speech has ancient origins. It was part of ancient Athens' political ideology (See Raaflaub, Ober, Wallace 2007). The Roman Empire also subscribed to it (See Charlesworth 1943).

England's Bill of Rights 1689 legally established the constitutional right of 'freedom of speech in Parliament' (Williams 1960). And during the French Revolution in 1789, Article 11 of the *Declaration of Rights of Man and the Citizen* stated that

> *The free communication of ideas and opinions is one of the most precious of the rights of man. Every citizen may, accordingly, speak, write, and print with freedom, but shall be responsible for such abuses of this freedom as shall be defined by law.*

But at the subjective/psychological/interpersonal level, it was Freud, as we observed previously, who put this into moment to moment practice, bringing a subjective fullness to the free speech principle, albeit within the confines of the psychoanalytic couch and the psychoanalytic hour.

The biggest problem with the free speech domain, as I see it, is that currently, it tends to be confined to one edge of the spectrum (the psychoanalytic hour) or the other (unrestrained global rants).

Wati Kanyilpai asks,

Dear reader, please give some thoughts and feelings to how we could manage the free speech domain in a caring and responsible way.

The global cultural evolutionary value of the concept and practice of developmental nurturance is the least obvious of our mega memes. And yet, in my view, its effective practice will make the difference between life and death on this planet. Explaining why this may be so is a core purpose of this book. In the next chapter, we will be looking at some of the attachment research and developmental neuroscience findings which shed light on the effects of nurturance and its failures. Please recall that no one can predict **absolute** outcome in any individual. But do also be aware that at the **group** level (groups of interest, organisations, societies, political systems, cultures), good studies **can** confidently predict population outcomes.

Not all megamemes are beneficial, and one darker fifth megameme needs to be mentioned in this discussion. We might call it the megameme of **hegemonic masculinity**, the cultural patterning that has underpinned male oppression for millennia.

The Fifth Megameme: Patriarchal Hegemony, Toxic Masculinity

There must have been a time in human history when women were in charge. But that was very long ago. The world's oldest living culture, indigenous Australia, has been around for at least sixty thousand years, and it is very patriarchal.

Wati Kanyilpai wants to remedy this. His yearning is to nurture the nurturers.

We all start life as foetuses in our mothers' wombs. Our fathers can be great nurturers, but they do not have wombs. In those first nine months of life in our mother's uterus, there are massive developments in brain function. The amygdala, the brain's alert system, comes online at six months, and the right hemisphere begins to develop its capacity for emotion and relationship. Maternal stress registers massively in the baby's developing brain programmes, generating damage.

We therefore need to support and nurture expectant mothers, for their sakes, and for the sakes of the babies. That is what Wati Kanyilpai encourages.

Hegemonic patriarchy is a term that was first developed and described many years ago by Raewyn Connell (Connell 1980), an Australian sociologist (currently professor emeritus for sociology in Sydney University). Raewyn Connell's personal history is very interesting and relevant. She is a transgender woman who completed her gender transition relatively late in life.

Raewyn defines *hegemonic masculinity* as a practice that legitimizes men's dominant position in society and justifies the subordination of women. In Raewyn's perspective, it is based on (1) domination of women and (2) a hierarchy of intermale dominance.

It manifests in high degree of ruthless competition, an inability to express emotions other than anger, an unwillingness to admit weakness or dependency, devaluation of women and all feminine attributes in men, and homophobia.

We would add a third foundational component of hegemonic masculinity, (3) the absolute lack of any sense of nurturance.

This kind of masculinity is of course the very opposite of what Watikanyilpai considers worthwhile.

Please be aware that when we talk about hegemonic masculinity, we are not censuring the many positive aspects of what is commonly regarded as masculinity—qualities like courage, resourcefulness, determination, and forcefulness. Nelson Mandela is a good example of a human being who combined these qualities with a deep reservoir of nurturance. It must be said though, that there are very few characteristics that are gender-specific, apart from the ability of the female womb to cultivate us in those first nine months of life.

Patriarchal/masculist culture is so deeply woven into the fabric of our day to day lives that it is often difficult to discern. It is here that writers like Clementine Ford (Ford 2018), in her painful analysis of the embedded/tacit/implicit aspects of hegemonic masculinity, can help us become more aware, a first step towards positive change. She reminds us how some men's mentality is so mindlessly embedded in masculine privilege they will react angrily to women's complaints of male violence along the lines, 'But only 0.5 per cent of men are rapists. The rest of us are not like that. Don't put us in the same basket,' when what is required is an acknowledgement of the evil, expressions of empathy for the victims, and commitments to protect the vulnerable.

Clementine reminds us that underneath the gross physical and sexual violence that characterises toxic masculinity, there are some subtler but equally toxic features that are so deeply woven into the fabric of our day-to-day lives, it is often difficult to discern them. Indeed, much of this was not fully apparent to me, a therapist and mindfulness meditator, for God's sake, until I read Clementine Ford's alarming book. Here are some of them.

1. 'A woman's place'—unpaid cleaning, feeding, minding, nurturing.
2. The condescending patronising way women (as opposed to men) are often portrayed (and employed) in films and the media.
3. The toxicity deniers . . . Ford cites Twitter user @ thetrudz who puts its essence well: 'Not all men are actual rapists. Some are rape apologists. Some tell rape jokes. Some are victim blamers. Some are silent.'

For the Women Reading this Book: This Is Especially for You

Hegemonic masculinity manifests in so many poisonous ways. It is not confined to the male gender. Women, of course, can be its proponents, as well as its victims.

Women often find themselves attracted to males with brutal narcissistic and sadistic traits. Research scientist Gregory Carter and his colleagues (Carter 2013) found that more men than women possess the 'dark triad' personality traits of narcissism, psychopathy, and Machiavellianism.

Narcissism includes dominance, a sense of entitlement, and a grandiose self-view. Studies overwhelmingly show that narcissism is greater in men, even across cultures. Narcissism involves 'a willingness and ability to compete with one's own sex, and to repel mates shortly after intercourse'. The authors note that narcissists are adept at beginning new relationships and identifying multiple mating opportunities. They are also less monogamous.

Psychopathy carries callousness and a lack of empathy. It too lends itself to success in short-term mating, through a moral deficit and interpersonal hostility. Psychopaths have also been found to exhibit superficial charm, deceit, and a sexually exploitative interpersonal stance.

Machiavellianism carries duplicity, insincerity, and extraversion. The manipulative, coercive, and opportunistic ways of these individuals are also advantageous in short-term mating. Machiavellians have been found to be more promiscuous.

Carter's study is part of a growing body of research unveiling women's duelling desires. On the one hand, they express wanting a relationship with a loving and committed partner for the long term. Yet on the other hand, they demonstrate an attraction to men with darker personalities, typically for the short term. It is important to recognize, however, that this dynamic has been shaped by the demands of *evolution*. For the women who fall for bad boys—and the men who love them—these insights may help untangle this paradox.

In their study, Carter and colleagues discovered that women found the dark triad personality more attractive than the control. This result is in keeping with previous studies in which dark triad men reported their increased level of sexual success. What might explain this result? Carter and colleagues offer two possible explanations.

First, women are responding to signals of 'male quality' when it comes to reproduction. And with respect to short-term mating, women may be drawn to bad boys, who demonstrate confidence, stubbornness, and risk-taking tendencies.

Second, *sexual conflict* in themselves—a useful tactic in a co-evolutionary 'arms race', in which men convince women to pursue the former's preferred sexual strategy. They note that like a used-car dealer, dark triad men may be effective charmers and manipulators, furthering their success at short-term mating. The authors are also careful to note that though women rated the DT character as comparatively more attractive, it does not necessarily mean that they would have sex with them.

This study is part of a growing body of research unveiling women's duelling desires. On the one hand, they express wanting a relationship with a loving and committed partner for the long term. Yet this dynamic has been shaped by the other factor: an attraction to men with darker personalities, typically for the demands of evolution. For the women who fall for bad boys—and the men who love these women, these insights may help untangle this paradox.

Computational neuroscientists Ogi Ogas and Sai Gaddam (Ogas and Gaddam 2011) have found substantial evidence from web searches, posts, and thousands of romance novels that women demonstrate a strong erotic preference for dominant men, what's commonly referred to as alpha males—in the authors' words, men who are 'strong, confident, [and] swaggering'. But this arrangement is often so self-centred and insensitive as to cross the line into physical, mental, and emotional abuse.

Consciously, most women would like their men to be kind, empathic, understanding and respectful. But there's something in the native wiring, the evolutionary genetics that makes a great many of them susceptible to 'bad boys'.

Much of this might well go back to prehistoric times when it was crucial that women choose mates who could defend them from various external threats. In today's society, women typically are far more independent and have the freedom to choose a partner based primarily on mental and emotional (versus physical or material) needs. But if their hardwiring predisposes them to be attracted to alpha males, modern-day rationality can still be offset by primordial instincts having little or nothing to do with reason. And, frankly, as a therapist I've encountered many women who bemoaned their vulnerability towards dominant men.

There is also a final important underlying factor: developmental trauma.

Developmental Trauma

When a female child has been exposed to a range of physical, emotional, and sexual abuses, she will be driven to connect with dysfunctional males. Part of the agenda will be to 'rescue' through love. Studies of women who get together with serial killers show that many of them feel that they can find sensitive and vulnerable cores in their partners and want to heal them through love. Professor **Katherine Ramsland** (DeSales University, Pennsylvania) discusses this in detail in her blog (2018).

Unfortunately, this rescue project seldom works. The love object is too damaged and simply takes an entitled attitude to the love offered.

Christine Armstrong (2018), in her recent book *The Mother of All Jobs*, focuses on the struggle women have in coping with the conflicting demands of child-rearing and career. Hegemonic masculinity devalues a woman's contribution to the former and oppresses a woman in her roles in the latter. The few exceptions to this are from women who have risen to very high organisational levels and can thus afford nannies and are less subject to oppression at work. But there is a price which is often quite unrecognised. This is the internalisation, into the women's' lives, of some of those hegemonic masculinity patterns and behaviours.

One final remark about hegemonic masculinity. Recently, in Australia, at a time when there was a national debate about same-sex marriage, an Anglican priest, Father Rod Bower, posted a street sign outside his church, saying *'Dear Christians, some people are gay. Get over it. Love, God'*. Soon after, thousands of death threats from trolls began to appear on social media. Some conservative Christians were outraged that he would dare support LGBTI people. He found himself embroiled in this campaign and wrote a book about his experience (Bower 2018). Do read it.

In summary, hegemonic masculinity has been around since caveman days and is in clear conflict with our four other megamemes, especially that of ***the centrality of early nurturance in human development***. Wati Kanyilpai promotes **nurturant** masculinity and encourages my fellow men and me to engage with the Wati Kanyilpai Dreaming project to remedy the situation, to step beyond hegemony.

In the next chapter, we move from the global perspective to the latest research findings in developmental neuropsychology and attachment theory that highlight the crucial importance of nurturance of those first three years of life.

BIBLIOGRAPHY

Armstrong, C. (2018). *The Mother of All Jobs: How to Have Children and a Career and Stay Sane(ish).* Bloomsbury.

Bower, R. (2018). *Outspoken: The Life and Work of the Man Behind Those Signs.* Edbury.

Bowlby, R., King, P. (2004). *Fifty Years of Attachment Theory: Recollections of Donald Winnicott and John Bowlby.* Karnac Books. p. 17. *ISBN 9781855753853.*

Carter, G. L. (2013). *Dark Triad Narcissism.* Elsevier Ltd.

Charlesworth, M. P. (1943). "Freedom of Speech in Republican Rome". *The Classical Review* (The Classical Association). **57** (1): 49. doi:10.1017/s0009840x 00311283.

Connell, R. W., Irving, T. H. (1980). *Class Structure in Australian History.* Longman Cheshire, Melbourne, 1980.

Dadds, M. R., Allen, J. L., Oliver, B. R., Faulkner, N., Legge, K., Moul, C., Woolgar, M., Scott, S. (2012). 'Love, Eye Contact and the Developmental Origins of Empathy v. Psychopathy.' *The British Journal of Psychiatry.* March. 200 (3) 191-196; DOI: 10.1192/bjp.bp.110.085720.

Dawkins, R. (1989). *The Selfish Gene.* Oxford University Press, ISBN 0-19-286092-5.

Fallon, J. (2013). *The Psychopath Inside: A Neuroscientist's Personal Journey into the Dark Side of the Brain.* Penguin Group USA LLC: New York.

Ford, Clementine. (2018). *Boys Will Be Boys.*

Raaflaub, K., Ober, J., Wallace, R. (2007). *Origins of Democracy in Ancient Greece.* University of California Press. p. 65. ISBN 0-520-24562-8.

Ramsland, Katherine (2018). Https://www.psychologytoday.com/au/blog/shadow-boxing/201204/women-who-love-serial-killers.

Ogas, O., and Gaddam, S. (2011). *A Billion Wicked Thoughts: What the World's Largest Experiment Reveals about Human Desire.* New York, NY, US: Dutton/Penguin Books.

Williams, E. N. (1960). *The Eighteenth-Century Constitution, 1688–1815.* Cambridge University Press. pp. 26–29. OCLC 1146699.

CHAPTER 3

Advances in Developmental Neuroscience: A Brief Overview

Failures of nurturance and failures of secure attachment for children in those vital first three years of life have awful consequences that spread from the child to larger society. Yet it wasn't until the child psychiatrist Dr John Bowlby began, in the 1950s, to investigate the consequences of early relational deprivation that the scientific community took any interest in this vital subject. And even then, continual antagonism and controversy troubled the field.

However, we can now say with gratefulness that, since then, huge advances in developmental neuroscience research have been developed confirming Bowlby's fretful concerns.

The research has generated a massive literature base. And yet, despite this, recognition of the importance of this issue has yet to penetrate many organisational and political systems.

Let us therefore move into this field now with Wati Kanyilpai, whose nurturant nature recognizes the importance of developmental neuroscience and the way it helps us understand the processes of development we all undergo in our earliest years.

The overview that follows is not meant to be a definitive text but needs to be included to give the reader some sense of its scope, because it underpins the core argument that early processes impact strongly on our capacity for nurturance. The literature is huge, but there are some authoritative overviews available which we recommend further on.

Wati Kanyilpai encourages you at this point to notice if any resistances are emerging. Check into them gently and exploratively. What are the physical sensations that go with it? What are the emotions that come up? And thoughts, ideas, impulses, memories? Don't want to read too much scientific claptrap? And what does it have to do with the intensely emotional business of nurturance and attachment anyway? But persevere, please. The scientific method is what we use to distinguish between fact and fancy. Take your time, write down whatever comes up, and post it on the Watikanyilpai blog. And be aware that what you find may give you some inkling of the resistance that the wider society brings to this subject. And finally, as you bring kindly mindfulness to your own process, recognise that you have engaged in a bit of self-nurturance, a bit of Wati Kanyilpai activity.

The First Three Years of Life

We can remember very little of the first three years of our lives. And yet this is the time that the brain networks and brain programmes develop that will determine so much of how we function; our capacity for impulse control, mindfulness, empathy, and relationships. All this drives our behaviours, mostly below the level of conscious awareness. It influences who we choose as partners, how we treat ourselves and other beings, and ultimately, how we treat our planet and all that live in it.

If the beings who nurture our baby selves in those first three years can live in a safe and supportive environment and engage with us in a good enough way (they do not have to be perfect), we are likely to grow up to be beings who are at less risk of a huge range of physical and mental illnesses and predispositions to violence, and who can engage lovingly with the world.

If we suffer neglect and abuse during those early years, we are much more prone to physical and mental illnesses, and our capacity for self-awareness and impulse control is so damaged that we run a much higher risk of hurting ourselves and other people (self-damaging behaviours, domestic violence, criminality, terrorism, corporate greed, the list goes on and on).

Developmental neuroscience, the study of how all this occurs, has only been around for forty years or so in human history. But for the very first time ever, we are beginning to understand, at the neurobiological level, what makes for good nurturance and how to encourage it. We also have a better understanding of how bad nurturance damages us and how we can begin to heal some of the damage.

In this overview, we will focus on the research on emotional-social development rather than cognitive development, though the two are obviously interconnected. I will therefore not deal with a range of important *cognitive* developmental findings (the work of Piaget would be a good example). There is already a huge body of literature on the subject, and its contributions will be considered as part of the larger view as it is developed, but cognitive/intellectual processing has limitations when it comes to dealing with feelings and relationships.

This chapter presents a broad orienting overview of the emotional-social aspect of developmental neuroscience field.

Attachment Dynamic, Research, and Theory

We have already mentioned Bowlby's groundbreaking work on attachment processes. This emerged largely out of children's experiences of loss and abandonment around the period of the Second World War. These experiences and their consequences needed people like Bowlby to observe and document them and then promulgate their findings to a wider audience. There must have been thousands of times before in human history that huge cohorts of children had lost their parents, but what was different was that Bowlby's era combined a scientific perspective with the openness and freedom of expression that had been promoted by psychoanalysis. A range of other workers in turn became involved in developing attachment theory further. I mention some of them here, but this is not an exclusive list.

Attachment Dynamics

The Work of Mary Ainsworth

Mary Ainsworth was a leading protagonist in the development of Bowlby's work. She was a Canadian research psychologist who moved to London after the Second World War and joined Bowlby's research team at the Tavistock Clinic. Bowlby had already shown that comparison of disrupted mother–child bonds to normal mother–child relationship showed that a child's lack of a mother figure lead to adverse development effects, and Mary Ainsworth helped develop this further.

In 1954, Mary left the Tavistock Clinic to do research in Africa, where she conducted further longitudinal field studies of mother–infant interaction and began to document a range of patterns in attachment disruption. In 1965, she and her colleague Barbara Wittig designed an experimental set-up, the ISS (infant Strange Situation procedure), as a way of assessing individual differences in attachment behaviour by evoking the infants' reactions when encountering stress (Ainsworth and Wittig 1969).

In the Strange Situation procedure, the infant (usually around twelve months old) and their caregiver enter a pleasant laboratory with objects and toys that the infant can play with. A person unknown to the infant then enters the room and slowly tries to connect with the child. The mother then leaves the room. The child is now alone with the stranger, and their response to that is observed, as is the response to the mother when she returns to the room. The observer can watch the infant: the interplay of exploration and attachment behaviour in the presence and or the absence of the parent. Initially, Mary Maine and her co-workers described two types of attachment behaviour or attachment dynamic: secure (65 per cent of a US sample) and insecure (35 per cent of a US sample). Further work by them in Baltimore unpacked the insecure group into two subgroups: avoidant/resistant and ambivalent/anxious. These will now be further described.

Secure Attachment

A child who's securely attached to its mother will explore freely while the principal caregiver (usually the mother) is present, using her as a safe base from which to explore. The child will engage with the stranger when the mother is present and will be visibly upset when the mother departs but happy to see her on her return. After a brief period of engagement with the mother, the child feels secure enough to return to play activities. As we mentioned before, studies show that about 45–65 per cent of US middle-class babies present with secure attachment.

Avoidant Insecure Attachment

Some 20–30 per cent of the US infant sample typically behaved as if neither the loss of the caregiver nor her return mattered. They just got on with self-contained activity, displaying what one might call premature autonomy. Further research showed that the primary caregiver, while good at providing basics like food and order and cleanliness, was not capable of much empathic resonance; and failed to pay much attention to the child's inner life and emotions.

Anxious–Ambivalent–Resistant Insecure Attachment

The children classified as anxious–ambivalent/resistant (some 10–15 per cent of the US samples) typically showed distress even before separation and were clingy and difficult to comfort on the caregiver's return, refusing to return to playing with the toys. They either showed signs of resentment in response to the absence (C1 subtype) or signs of helpless passivity (C2 subtype). The parental style tended to be either inconsistent (sometimes tuned-in, sometimes not) and/or intrusive, pushing the parent's agenda at the expense of the infant's process in the moment.

Mary Main and Disorganised Attachment

Mary Main is an American psychologist who has done remarkable work in the field of attachment. She is currently a professor at the University of California, Berkeley. Mary Main was among the first doctoral students who worked with Mary Ainsworth at the Johns Hopkins University in Baltimore, exploring the relationship between attachment and infant play in her doctoral research. Main, together with Ainsworth, found that infants who were securely attached to their mothers engaged in more exploration and interactive play. Important aspects of Main's early work also included developing a scale for avoidant infant behaviour.

Insecure-avoidance, which Mary Ainsworth and Mary Main worked on together, is coded using a 1–7 scale for 'avoidance'. Whereas infants classified as secure would seek their caregiver on reunion, show their distress, and receive comfort, 'avoidance' was a measure of the extent to which an infant kept their attention away from their caregiver and avoided showing their distress. Main conceptualised avoidance as a 'conditional behavioural strategy'. Whilst it might seem odd or maladaptive at first sight for a child to turn away from their caregiver when anxious, Main argued from an evolutionary perspective that avoidance could be regarded as a strategy to achieve the protective proximity enjoined by the attachment system but which responds to the context of a caregiver who would rebuff them and be less protective.

But most significantly, in 1986 Mary Main, together with Judith Solomon, introduced a new infant attachment classification, 'disorganized/disoriented' (D), for the Ainsworth Strange Situation procedure (Main and Solomon 1986, 1990), based on a review of discrepant infant behaviours in the Strange Situation.

Disorganized/Disoriented Attachment

This fourth category featured in about 5 per cent of various US samples. In 1990, Ainsworth put in print her blessing for the new D classification, though she urged that the addition be regarded as 'open-ended, in the sense that subcategories may be distinguished', as she worried that the D classification might be too encompassing and might subsume too many different forms of behaviour (Duchinsky 2015). In contrast to infants in other categories classified by Mary Ainsworth, who present a standard path of reactions while dealing with the stress of separation and reunion, type D infants appeared to possess no set pattern of coping mechanism. In fact, these infants had mixed features such as "strong proximity seeking followed by strong avoidance or appeared dazed and disoriented upon reunion with their caretakers (or both)'. A large range of studies investigated this phenomenon, and there is a huge body of literature on the subject: see for example Bernier et al, De Oliveira, and Lyons-Ruth (Bernier and Meins 2008, De Oliveira et al. 2004, Lyons-Ruth 2007, Lyons-Ruth et al. 2013).

The principal carers typically displayed frightening behaviours or else carried high levels of fear themselves. And they often behaved in a confusing manner. The message the infant got was one of a fearful or frightening carer to whom it was impossible to turn for comfort. This had a powerful negative impact on the development of emotional regulation.

Project STEEP (Studying Teacher Effectiveness, Education, and Policy), a school-based investigation, showed that infants that were presented with disorganized/disoriented (type D) patterns, tested with higher cortisol concentrations in saliva than infants in the traditional (ABC) classifications, a sign of chronic stress (Duschinsky 2015).

In general, disorganized behaviours occur only briefly before the infant then enters back into one of the Ainsworth A, B, or C attachment patterns. As such, infants coded as disorganized/disoriented are also given a secondary A, B, or C classification (Lyons-Ruth and Jacobvitz 2008). The discrepant behaviours are most often exhibited on reunion but are found in other episodes of the procedure as well.

Main and Solomon developed a set of thematic headings for the various forms of disorganized/disoriented behaviour. Infant behaviours coded as disorganized/disoriented include sequential display of contradictory behaviour patterns (index I); simultaneous display of contradictory behaviour patterns (II); undirected, misdirected, incomplete, and interrupted movements and expressions (III); stereotypies, asymmetrical movements, mistimed movements, and anomalous postures (IV); freezing, stilling, and slowed movements and expressions (V); direct indices of apprehension regarding the parent (VI); direct indices of disorganization or disorientation (VII) (Main and Solomon 1990).

Like the Ainsworth classifications, disorganized/disoriented attachment with one caregiver does not necessarily predict the classification with another caregiver. You may have noticed this yourself in some of your relations with children. This implies that the classification is tapping a quality of the relationship and not merely the child's temperament (van Ijzendoorn et al. 1999).

A classification of disorganized/disoriented attachment has been found to be a particularly severe risk factor for later development (Sroufe et al. 1999). For example, this classification in infancy has been found associated with school-age externalising problem behaviour (van Ijzendoorn et al. 1999, Fearon et al. 2010, Carlson 1998, Ogawa et al. 1997) and development of post-traumatic stress symptoms following trauma exposure (McDonald et al. 2008). Behaviours associated with disorganization have been found to undergo transformation from the age of two and typically develop into various forms of well-organised controlling behaviour towards the parent. Some children are overly solicitous and protective towards the parent (classified by Main and Cassidy as controlling-caregiving), while others are harshly directive or rudely humiliating towards the parent (classified controlling-punitive) (Main and Cassidy 1988, Moss et al. 2004).

Assessing Attachment Patterns and Predicting Capacity for Good Nurturance

The Adult Attachment Inventory looks at how the attachment patterns that an adult demonstrates while they are performing the test interview.

Unlike in the Strange Situation (which assesses an infant's attachment security to a particular person), the Adult Attachment Interview does not assess attachment security with respect to any specific past or current relationship but instead evaluates an individual's overall state of mind with respect to attachment. A person can be without a secure attachment to any other living person in their current situation but still have a secure-autonomous state of mind with respect to attachment.

AAI responses can be:

- coherent and collaborative (interacts well with their inner life, early biographic memory, and the interviewer),
- dismissive (lack of recall and no supportive memories),
- preoccupied (entangled, past intrudes into present, sometimes intense idealisations),
- unresolved (grief or trauma, impaired neural integration, searching memory and maintaining reciprocal discourse).

Interviewees categorised as *secure-autonomous* display a coherent and collaborative nature. The interviewees appear to be balanced and objective in their descriptions and evaluations of relationships and overall seem to value attachment.

Interviews categorised as ***dismissing*** display inconsistent descriptions and evaluations of relationships. The interviewees may claim to have had positive attachment relationships and experiences but provide unconvincing or contradictory evidence to support this or acknowledge negative experiences but insist these experiences have had little effect or only made them stronger.

Interviews categorised as ***preoccupied*** are characterised by angry, vague, confused, or fearful fixation on particular attachment relationships or experiences.

Performance on the Adult Attachment Inventory (AAI) turns out to be better than observation of the same adult in Strange Situation interactions with their infant, in terms of predicting what the child's attachment style will turn out to be several years later! Parent AAI predicts 85 per cent of child attachment styles, versus infant Strange Situation or other parent–child interactions' 75 per cent (Main, Hesse, Kaplan 2005) because it explores mentalisation/mindsight, which is largely absent in a video. Does this take you by surprise? Understanding one's own childhood history (when the parent's AAI produces *coherent* narratives, as opposed to cohesive narratives, i.e. 'plausible' accounts manufactured for some other benefit) best predict how adequately you will parent your own children and whether the child will have a secure attachment to that particular parent. The left hemisphere generates the linear narrative. The right hemisphere generates limbic/ emotional plus autobiographic memory plus mindsight. And good interhemispheric communication produces interpersonal integration, which in turn activates *neural* integration, allowing for a *coherent* narrative.

Why Are Attachment Patterns Important? A Summary

Attachment patterns are largely independent of genetics. Genetics contributes to temperament but not attachment style, which is shaped by early experiences with caregivers.

A child typically needs and benefits from several attachment figures. Srouf (1993), Srouf and Siegel (2011), and Hrdy (2009) detail these points well. This was the norm in Australian Aboriginal cultures until the traditional kinship networks were influenced by Western mores. In our Western world, there is a growing trend towards single-parent families isolated from grandparents and uncles and aunts. This can put huge pressures on the nurturer and, in turn, the nurtured infant.

We also know that attachment styles play a significant role in romantic relationships and partner choice (Mikulincer and Shaver 2007). Unfortunately, people with attachment trauma tend to be drawn to problem partners. For instance, women with a background of childhood abuse and driven by right-brain limbic relationship programmes often find themselves in relations with abusive partners, with painful consequences for the children, who in turn grow up to repeat the cycle, feeding a cascade of transgenerational dysfunction.

These right-brain limbic programmes are preverbal and thus not easily accessible to introspection. The details of this have been thoroughly researched by leading developmental neuroscientist Alan Schore (2003, 2008, 2012) whose theoretical work focuses on the enduring effect of early trauma on brain development. Schore has used neuroimaging research methodology to investigate these phenomena, and his work is discussed further in the section on neuroimaging below.

In summary, there are four kinds of attachment patterns: secure (around 65 per cent), avoidant (20 per cent), anxious (10 per cent), and disorganised (5 per cent). The last is associated with high degrees of psychological, social, and metabolic pathology, and a range of dissociation symptoms (Sroufe 1999). Many of the children in this last category would have a *DSM-5* diagnosis of reactive attachment disorder.

Reactive Attachment Disorder and Developmental Trauma Disorder: Two Strong Categorisations

These two diagnostic terms are used to refer to the damage that occurs when the baby/infant's early nurturance needs are not met properly, for whatever reason.

The first term, reactive attachment disorder, refers to the severest form of disturbance, and it is the term we would use to describe what happened, for instance, to the Romanian orphans.

In the mid '60s, Romanian dictator Nicole Ceausescu passed laws which resulted in a huge influx of babies into state orphanages. These were grotesquely overcrowded and understaffed. The children suffered gross neglect and physical and sexual abuse. They were left with severe intellectual and social-emotional impairments. The features of RAD include markedly disturbed and developmentally inappropriate social relatedness in most contexts (e.g. the child is avoidant or unresponsive to care when offered by caregivers or else is indiscriminately affectionate with strangers) (Solomon and George 2011). The pattern of behaviour of such a child in the Strange Situation procedure would fit into the highly disorganised category.

DSM-IV and *5* define reactive attachment disorder along the following criteria:

- The disturbance is not accounted for solely by developmental delay.
- The onset has to be before five years of age.
- There is a history of significant neglect.
- There is an implicit lack of identifiable, preferred attachment figure.

But there is a larger range of somewhat less severe, but still very troubling conditions caused by lesser forms of early neglect or abuse (For instance: the mother might be suffering from post-partum depression and does not have any supportive relatives who can care for and bond with the baby, or the baby may go through an adequate first three or four years of nurturance but be sexually abused by a family member at this later stage). One term proposed by the psychiatrist Judith Herman to cover this much more common set of conditions was 'complex (or developmental) post-traumatic stress disorder', because the term referred both to experiences of serial abuse (as opposed to the more usual single exposures to horrific life-threatening incidents in the more usual PTSD) and their occurrence at a stage when the brain was still in the process of development, resulting in different symptom patterns to the ones seen in PTSD resulting from trauma in adulthood.

Director of the National Centre for Child Traumatic Stress Complex Trauma Network (NCTSN) Bessel van der Kolk and his team (van der Kolk 2005, van der Kolk et al. 2009) proposed the term 'developmental trauma disorder' to cover much the same ground as 'complex PTSD', but extend it to a wider range of developmental nurturance failures. They ran a survey of 40,000 children being treated nationwide for multiple traumas. 'Most of them do not meet the criteria for PTSD . .

. as the majority of issues are not specific traumas, but *issues in their attachment relationships.'*

Bessel reviews the field very eloquently. To encourage you to read his book *The Body Keeps the Score* (van der Kolk 2014), I include some extracts from the opening paragraphs of his 2005 proposal 'Developmental Trauma Disorder: Towards a Rational Diagnosis for Children with Complex Trauma Histories'.

> *Childhood trauma, including abuse and neglect, is probably our nation's single most important public health challenge, a challenge that has the potential to be largely resolved by appropriate prevention and intervention. Each year over 3,000,000 children are reported to the authorities for abuse and/or neglect in the United States of which about one million are substantiated. Many thousands more undergo traumatic medical and surgical procedures, and are victims of accidents and of community violence (see Spinazzola et al, this issue). However, most trauma begins at home: the vast majority of people (about 80%) responsible for child maltreatment are children's own parents . . . Research has shown that traumatic childhood experiences are not only extremely common; they also have a profound impact on many different areas of functioning. For example, children exposed to alcoholic parents or domestic violence rarely have secure childhoods; their symptomatology tends to be pervasive and multifaceted, and is likely to include depression, various medical illnesses, as well as a variety of impulsive and self-destructive behaviors. Approaching each of these problems piecemeal, rather than as expressions of a vast system of internal disorganization runs the risk of losing sight of the forest in favor of one tree.*

Van der Kolk also contends, quite correctly in my view, that it is at the root of **borderline personality disorder** and **bipolar disorder** and many cases misdiagnosed as **ADHD/ADD**.

Van der Kolk and his team proposed the DTD diagnosis to the American Psychiatric Association and the *DSM-5* diagnostic handbook committee, but they rejected it. This resonates with my often repeated point that professional and political organisations seem to display a selective blindness to nurturance issues.

As we mentioned earlier, except for the most severe forms of RAD, attachment patterns with one caregiver do not necessarily transfer fully to another caregiver. It is quite possible, for instance, to have a relatively secure pattern with the mother and a much more anxious one with the father. This has useful implications for therapy, and I need to share with the reader that the patients in my private psychotherapy practice *all* have DTD to some degree, and my principal first task is to develop a secure attachment dynamic with them.

Abuse comes in many forms. There is the violent lashing out that we see in people with poor impulse control. And we know that poor impulse control is a consequence of early abuse.

But there is also the cruelty and exploitation that we see in psychopathy and sociopathy. This may not involve physical violence but can have disastrous consequences nevertheless. However, the matter is further complicated by the fact that psychopathy seems to have a genetic basis, as we mentioned earlier. As we mentioned earlier, studies by Dadds and others (Dadds et al. 2012, Fallon 2013) show that a child with a genetic loading for psychopathy can be helped with eye contact and mindfulness and empathy therapies/practices. By and large, families of children with psychopathic behavioural issues '*tend to be pretty good parents: motivated, engaged and loving, not high rates of abuse . . . The evidence so far is this is not something we can blame on the parents,'* as Dadds says (2011). But a dysfunctional nurturer will not only be unwilling/unable to implement various treatment programmes but may make the psychopathic child's impulse control even worse.

Neuroimaging Studies: How Recent Advances in Developmental Neuroscience Can Help Inform Our Understanding of the Impact of Early Nurturance

As we moved into the eighties, a range of technologies emerged that had not been available for Bowlby and his colleagues. They all in their various ways essentially allowed us to get glimpses into the working brain (or the workings of the autonomic nervous system). They include techniques like the measurement of heart rate variability (HRV, a window into the dynamic of the autonomic nervous system) and a range of neuroimaging resources which can provide not only still pictures but ones of the brain in action. Some of them include technologies with acronyms like PET, fMRI, SPECT, QEEG, MEEG.

These technologies have been used to look at what was happening in the brains of mums and their babies, even when the babies were in the womb.

FMRI (functional magnetic resonance imagery) tracks the areas of the brain that become oxygenated (i.e. become more active) in relation to various mind states and activities. It has good spatial resolution (better than one cubic centimetre), but its time resolution is poorer, down to about two seconds. Several years ago, I used fMRI to look at what happens when a person's complexes get activated. Subjects performed a word association test while in the MRI machine (Petchkovsky, L.,

Petchkovsky, M., et al. 2013). Usually, the response is rapid and commonplace. The stimulus word *dog* will produce a response like *cat* within a second or two. But sometimes, something unusual will occur. The response to *dog* could be similar to *my mother* instead and take seven or eight seconds. A complex has been activated, and when we ask the person to unpack, it emerges that their mother used to growl angrily at them in childhood. The fMRI results show that the right-hemisphere limbic system gets activated, especially the middle cingulate gyrus area and the anterior insula, areas that are known to light up when we experience emotional pain either in ourselves or in someone we empathise with.

QEEG (quantitative EEG) is another interesting brain imaging technology. Its spatial resolution is poorer than that of the fMRI (both in terms of precision and reliability), but its temporal resolution is in the microsecond range! I have used this technology more frequently. It is much cheaper and more office-friendly. A study we did (Petchkovsky, Robertson-Gillam, et al. 2013) on the impact of a choir singing programme on depression showed some interesting results. The P3a response (a brain response that occurs within about three hundred milliseconds after an unexpected stimulus and when excessive is an index of chronic pathological hypervigilance), which was in the pathological range before the treatment, reduced to normal levels afterwards!

This book is not about the technical details of various brain-imaging procedures, but it does look at findings, both of how the brain functions normally and in dysfunctional attachment patterns and developmental trauma.

Do Google these technologies if you want to find more scientific details. I suspect you will enjoy it.

Some Major Research and Researchers in These Areas

Allan Schore, Dan Siegel, Louis Cozolino, and Bessel van der Kolk are just a few of the wonderful researchers in this new era, and I recommend Alan Schore's *Affect Regulation and the Repair of the Self* (2003), Dan Siegel's *Mindsight* (2011), Louis Cozolino's *The Neuroscience of Human Relationships* (2014), and Bessel van der Kolk's *The Body Keeps the Score* (2014), for readers who want to learn still more about the science behind our new understanding of the processes and consequences of developmental trauma and the methods of repair.

Another detailed and comprehensive overview can be found in the aptly named *The Impact of Early Life Trauma on Health and Disease: The Hidden Epidemic* (Lanius, Vermetten, and Pain 2010).

During the nine months we spend in the uterus, a range of stressors will have a powerful negative impact on brain development, and Kathleen Gyllenhaal (2015) has produced a good film on the subject, using neuropsychologist Gabor Mate's work in this field. Look it up on https://kindredmedia. org/2015/06/an-interview-with-in-utero-filmmaker-kathleen-gyllenhaal-includes-podcast-and-transcript/.

Brain Findings in Nurturance Failure

What has emerged is a recognition that a range of nurturance failures (domestic violence, neglect, physical and sexual abuse, poor emotional attunement) produce a wide range of brain changes and failures of development in the baby. The neurodevelopmental results of early stress and abuse are grim: brain states of chronic hyperarousal and attachment dysfunction.

Dysregulation of a range of body–brain systems follows, including (1) the hormonal system, the hypophyseal pituitary adrenal (HPA) axis (Cozolino, 269–73, and Meaney 2001); (2) the autonomic nervous system, with special reference to a failure of development of the myelinated vagus, which helps down-regulate overactive sympathetic adrenal hyperarousal (Porges 2011); (3) the limbic system, especially the right amygdala (Siegel 2011, Schore 2003); and (4) the resonance circuitry that is implicated in attachment dynamics, mindfulness (awareness of self-processes), and empathy (awareness of the other). In the first two years of life (including the intrauterine period), neocortical areas, especially in the right hemisphere, undergo massive neurodevelopmental changes (Siegel 2011, Schore 2003). The right hemisphere mediates attachment patterns and dynamics, as well as wariness of danger. Alan Schore's metaphor puts it succinctly. The infant downloads the mother's right prefrontal programmes into their own right prefrontal area. And if the mother's paralimbic emotional-relational programmes are problematic, then so are the child's. This programming is preverbal, and even though it has a profound influence on our behaviour, especially how we get on with others, it is not directly accessible to introspection or easily influenced by verbal interventions.

Bessel van der Kolk's term *developmental trauma disorder* covers the territory well (van der Kolk 2009). Its symptomatology includes (1) chronic dysthymia (we are easily upset, feel miserable a lot of the time), (2) vulnerability to substance abuse (we needs alcohol or drugs to dull the pain), (3) a range of attention deficit hyperactivity symptoms, which contribute to (4) educational retardation (we do badly even if we are very bright) (5) poor impulse control (we lash out at ourselves and others), (5) various attachment disorders (difficult to give and receive nurturance even though we desperately need it), and (7) a generalised reduction in physical and psychological resilience. There are also serious physical consequences like metabolic syndrome, a consequence of the disturbed hormonal HPA axis function we mentioned earlier, with its weight problems, proneness to cardiovascular disease and diabetes and reduced life expectancy, and increased incidence of autoimmune diseases. We have known for a long time that CD45RO, a gene whose expression facilitates T cells, is reduced in PTSD and DTD. Hence lots of auto immune disorders like multiple sclerosis can result. Impaired T cells react as if body is in constant danger (van der Kolk et al. 1999).

Metabolic and immunity factors interact with neuropsychological ones in a vicious feedback circle.

I strongly recommend Maclean Hospital developmental researcher Martin Teicher's powerful recent overviews of this subject, (Teicher et al. 2016, 2015). As he reminds us, *'Maltreatment-related childhood adversity is the leading preventable risk factor for mental illness and substance abuse'*.

As if that is not grave enough, we now know that poor nurturance can also affect a range of genes involved in brain development and brain function in ways which allow these modifications to pass on to further generations (epigenetics), independently of the quality of the environment. Meaney and his colleagues at McGill University have done some of the leading research on the epigenetic process in animals and humans (Meaney 2001, McGowan 2009).

The Financial Costs of Childhood Maltreatment

Our political systems need to be aware of this. Fang and co-workers (2012) published an estimate of the economic cost of childhood maltreatment in the US. They estimated the total burden to be as large as $585 billion.

This is discussed in greater detail in our final chapter.

Damaged Nurturers

Abuse and neglect during those vital first three years of life produces a multitude of problematic consequences. As if that were not bad enough, we now know (as mentioned earlier) that damaged nurturers, even when they try very hard to be good parents, can still pass on their problematic attachment dynamics to their children in the first two or so years of life, resulting in yet another generation of people with avoidant, anxious/ambivalent, and disorganised attachment patterns.

The developmental neuroscientist Ruth Lanius and her colleagues have compiled their research findings in their comprehensive book *Healing the Traumatised Self* (Frewen and Lanius 2015), which I strongly recommend. In my connections with Ruth, via my mentor Sebern Fisher, I learnt that Ruth had done some important studies on the default mode network (DMN) in children of traumatised mothers.

The idling state of the brain is mediated by the DMN, when a person is not focused on the outside world and the brain is in wakeful rest. It activates by default when a person is not involved in a task. It mediates a sense of self. DMN defects are involved in dissociative states.

The DMN develops throughout childhood and only matures in late adolescence. Ruth Lanius and her colleagues have found, in their brain-imaging studies, that adult patients of traumatised parents had developmentally retarded DMNs, which looked like those of seven- to nine-year-old children!

Ruth Buczynski is the president of the National Institute for the Clinical Application of Behavioural Medicine. The website of this organisation is http://www.nicabm.com/trauma-the-neurobiology-of-attachment-and-trauma/.

In their blog, a contributor, *Sara*, puts the matter very graphically.

I never thought of myself as having had trauma, but it is becoming clearer now that I have had and that it has negatively affected all my relationships. I have had three marriages to men who kept an emotional distance. My mother was a prescription drug addict and several times experienced insulin and electric shock therapy. After treatment she would look right through me without even seeing me. She was manic at home. I was so afraid of her in my teens that I slept with a knife under my pillow. When my son was born I loved him dearly but did not form an intimate bond. Or I did but I broke it off because feeling that close to another person frightened me that something was wrong. Many were the times I looked past him wishing the day would wear on. I thought I was raising him to be independent but I would withdraw support before he was ready. He, of course, never established bonds with others. He lost touch with his children. He learned to find solace in drugs with the other disconnected souls. Eventually he overdosed. I am depressed and dissociative and am losing touch with my granddaughters. Only now, after listening to your video [a Ruth Lanius video on this website], do I realize that my failure to be the parent I should have been may well have been beyond my conscious control. I would add here that my mother herself was never parented, having been removed from the home of an alcoholic mother and an absent alcoholic homeless father. There is no telling how many generations back the dissociation began. I recognize my place in this chain and do not have the

> *strength to stop it. A traumatized parent will produce a traumatized child who will as a traumatized parent produce a traumatized child who . . . So, there you have it.*

At this point, the topic becomes so painfully, excruciatingly contentious that it affects not only individuals and attitudes about overstressed single mothers and children at risk but public child protection policy, as Sammut and colleagues detail in their review of Australian child protection policies (Sammut 2015). Furthermore, mums with developmental trauma will typically be estranged from their families of origin because that is where they suffered abuse. And they will be instinctively driven to have babies to get some vicarious repair for themselves.

A range of researchers in the US and Australia have written that a key variable is family structure, with children in single-parent families most at risk, followed by stepfamilies, and those with traditional two biological parents least at risk. Two groups of Perth-based Australian researchers, LSAC (2013), and Sanson and colleagues (Sanson et al. 2002) have done some very important studies in this area but were driven by nervousness about offending the many people in ***nontraditional*** families who are doing a great job raising their children. They had been hoping their findings would slip under the media radar, and unfortunately, this seems to be what happened.

But we need to proceed with love and caution here. The whole point of the exercise is not to lay blame but to find ways of supporting/caring for the nurturers at risk, for their sake, for their children's sake, and for the planet's sake.

As we have said earlier, women with severe developmental trauma are exquisitely sensitive, struggle with impulse control, are chronically anxious and depressed, are often driven to get together with brutal dysfunctional partners, and feel compelled to get pregnant in an unconscious thrust to get some vicarious repair. Engaging in some sort of therapy is typically an impossible task. They feel so criticised and humiliated that they find it almost impossible to engage.

What Does Neuroscience Tell Us about Good Nurturance in Therapy and in Infancy?

Probably one of the most readable accounts of how recent neuroscience findings impact on the practice of psychotherapy is that developed by Dan Siegel and his colleagues (Siegel 2011). *Interpersonal neurobiology*, the term they use to designate their discipline, says it all. It is about the way our recent neuroscience advances help us understand what is happening both subjectively and *inter*subjectively. This, in turn, informs psychotherapy practice.

Anne Ashley (2016), a British Jungian analyst, puts the core of the matter succinctly in a post to *The Guardian* (http://www.theguardian.com/science/2016/jan/12/whether-to-pick-sides-in-psychology-today):

> *the treatment of emotional suffering through the medium of a reliable and benign relationship with another, has its roots in the simplest and most profound truth: a baby who has a mother who is emotionally available, loving and interested, has a better chance of growing up to be able to weather the storms of life without recourse to self-destructive (e.g. drug/alcohol dependency) responses.*

In the first few years of life, providing security is just the first essential step. The next step is to establish that as a base upon which the developmental dance of attunement may be enacted. But even this is not enough if the result is a limited empathy, an individual who may be functional but still identifies only with narrow tribal or sectarian concerns. A further step is needed, to do with enlarging the scope of mindful empathy. Let me try to unpack this for you.

Let us begin in the uterus, at five months to be precise. This is the time when the right amygdala, an almond-shaped nucleus which determines experiential salience, first comes online. Domestic violence lights it up, as do any other significant stresses on the mother (and the mother's amygdala). In both mother and baby, fear triggers a fight-or-flight response. If it is overwhelming, a frozen hopelessness ensues. Stressors less extreme will also activate safety and comfort-seeking clinging behaviour via the right amygdala's connections with other regions in the right prefrontal lobe, whereby the social engagement systems get activated. Caring responses will then pacify amygdalar overactivity, and, as a result of months and years of such experiences, memories/internal representations of comforting are laid down neurologically so that it becomes possible for the growing being to pacify itself in times of stress and thus gradually build resilience. What I've described is an (over)simplified version of the laying down of basic attachment states and behaviours to do with psychological resilience. This is the vital secure foundation for the next steps, those of developing a sense of self, developing a sense of other beings. These require the beautiful dance of interrelational attunement that we see between mums and babies when a secure base is in place. For the next few years, this neurodevelopmental dance goes on between infant and carer, and between the right amygdala and its to and fro connections with the rest of the (mainly) right brain, especially the middle anterior bits that have to do with emotional modulation and relational processes (to internal experience, experience of others, experience of the world). Alan Schore, probably the world's leading contemporary infant developmental researcher, puts it graphically: the programmes of the mother's right anterior lobe get downloaded into the baby's right anterior lobe, for good or ill.

Left-and-Right-Brain Tango

I am very fond of Iain McGilchrist's extraordinary book *The Master and His Emissary* (McGilchrist 2009), his take on the difference between left and right hemispheric function and how the hemispheres talk (or do not talk) with each other. My main critique of McGilchrist is that even though he is well aware of how those first three or so years of life determine how the right hemisphere will function (and thus the capacity of left and right to talk with each other meaningfully), he fails to enlarge on the importance of early nurturance. In essence, I want echo McGilchrist's 'interhemispheric dialogue' take on nurturing the nurturers, looking not just at developmental neuroscience and the impact of failed nurturance in indigenous and broader communities but looking at what religion, history, art, and politics say (and do not say) about the subject and why.

We are all right-brained creatures for the first two years, to such an extent that our right brain becomes, and remains, the larger of the two hemispheres, especially its anterior parts. The left hemisphere only begins to develop from the second year onwards. By and large the right hemisphere perceives experience as holistic and relational, but also fearful when pushed to its extremes. When you are a little creature in the jungle, the object of prey, you get into right-brain mode. You flee your attackers; you run to your protectors. Animal studies confirm this.

When you are in left-brain mode, the experiential mode is more linear, logical, and particulate, but it has an exploratory element, a curiosity, that becomes murderous when pushed to extremes—a predator mode.

Iain McGilchrist, in his book *The Master and His Emissary* (2014), reviews cutting-edge neurobiology research into hemisphericity, and its impact on history, art, culture, and politics. Each hemisphere of the brain has its way of being, a different take on the world, a different version of the world. 'The left hemisphere has its own agenda, to manipulate and use the world.' The right has a broader outlook, 'has no preconceptions, and simply looks out to the world for whatever might be', including protectors and predators. Right brain is relational but also apprehensive. Iain favours the notion that it is a good thing when left and right hemispheres are relating well with each because a third more integrative mode of awareness becomes possible.

Professor Jack Pettigrew (University of Queensland), one of Australia's leading neuroscientists, takes the role of hemisphericity further (Pettigrew and Miller 1998). He sees clinical mania as a state dominated by left hemisphericity, where predator mode has gone berserk, and is delusionally self-righteous. In depressive states, right hemispheric activities predominate. Jack advances some compelling neuroscience evidence for this. His website http://www.uq.edu.au/nuq/jack/jack.html is well worth visiting, especially his section on bipolar disorder, and 'sticky switch' theory, where he proposes that people with a genetic predisposition to BPAD tend to be born with a slower rate of interhemispheric switching than the norm and hence, as oscillator theory predicts, are more prone to get stuck in the left hemisphere and mania or in the right hemisphere and depression (see http://www.uq.edu.au/nuq/jack/BipolarDisorder.html).

I am condensing and oversimplifying enormously, but there is much convergence across neurobiology, animal ethology, and social psychology research to support these broad strokes and their experiential grounding.

In fact, you can try out some of this interhemispheric stuff for yourself. Look at which side a nursing mother holds her infant. The chances are it will be on her left, all the better to support maternal right-brain to infant right-brain communication, as recent studies confirm.

When you are with your dog or observing a crow in your backyard, note which eye orients towards you (remember left eye equals right-brain attention, and vice versa). Looking at you with her left eye (right brain), your dog is in relational mode, may want to give or receive some nurturing. Your crow, however, is less familiar with you, and her right brain could be in apprehension mode.

Now your companion's head orients to the right (right eye, left brain), and you are an object of curiosity and play. But if you are with a wolf and his right head (left brain) is looking at you too persistently, you'd better take cover—curiosity may be turning to predation.

But what does this have to do with nurturance? Again, put simply, the goodness of the dance of attunement between baby and carer depends on a base of security, and actually determines crucial aspects of brain development—in particular, capacity for self-monitoring, empathy, relationship, impulse control, theory of mind (the capacity to know and map the inner lives of other beings). All are themes well developed by UCLA child psychiatrist researcher Dan Siegel and his colleagues.

The actual brain wiring and the programmes that develop and get supported by this depend on nurturance. If attunement is consistent, left and right hemispheric functions will develop optimally. Good relationship between mother and child; good relationship between amygdala and prefrontal cortex. Once past infancy, and assuming you have had a good enough experience of nurturance, you are now neurologically equipped to develop broader connections with society and culture. This is paralleled by better quality left–right hemispheric attunement.

When things go wrong, the corpus callosum, the bridge between the left and right hemisphere, begins to shrink! Developmental neuroscientist Martin Teicher describes this well in his 2010 publication in the *American Journal of Psychiatry* (2010).

Patricia O'Rourke, a gifted baby and infant therapist at the Royal Adelaide Hospital, nurtures the nurturers. She helps women struggling to mother their babies and infants by bringing an experientially grounded sensitivity which draws on her deep experience of psychodrama, the most powerfully interactive of all the psychotherapies. She has written a thoughtful thesis on the links between nurturance, attunement processes, and psychodramatic modes of enactment. In essence, once a secure base has been established (for the baby in nurturance, for the protagonist in the psychodrama group), several mutually interactive processes can then be accessed, which will develop sense of self and other, greater capacity for self-tracking (mindfulness, if you will), greater empathy with others, and those experiences of vitality that we call play or spontaneity or creativity. Processes of healing and reparation emerge as all of the above goes on. Patricia distinguishes several processes common to the two domains. In the psychodrama, the protagonist is supported by the audience and a cast of actors. Their triple task is to mirror, double, and role-reverse. Mirroring or reflection by the group shows the protagonist what is going on for her. In doubling, one of the actors takes this further and immerses themselves in the protagonist's state of mind as a resonating 'twin' prepared to take her turmoil into their own being. In role reversal, this capacity for empathy extends further, as actors take on the roles of critical others in the protagonist's life (the mothers, husbands, children, friends, enemies, etc.). There is, of course, a parallel in the infant's nurturing process. A mother mirrors her baby when she matches her noises and movements so that the baby can receive something of herself and begin to build a sense of self. In doubling, she takes it further by resonating deeply with her baby's state of being. The baby can now get a sense of being deeply empathised with; she now has a companion who bounces with her joys and aches with her sorrows. Her developing awareness of self deepens because there is a sense of being kindly understood. Resilience is promoted as well as a dawning sense of the other as separate but loving. Later on, as the capacity for play and language increases and left and right brain begin to interact, both cognitive and emotional empathy can extend beyond the mother–infant pair to include others, paralleling the capacity for role reversal we see in psychodrama. Mistakes will be made, but they can also be repaired. This reparative reassurance moves the child beyond the Babylonian despot Hammurabi's famous code, a rigid universe of '*What once is written can never never be unwritten*'. Repair is now available to deal with the inevitable malfunctions that are part of life and relationships.

Coming from a different direction (self-psychology and the syntactic analysis of interactions between therapists and their patients, and mothers and their infants), Professor Russel Meares comes to similar conclusions. Theory of mind (the capacity for empathy) and the capacity for play / creativity / healthy spontaneity emerge through good quality nurturance. His classic *The Metaphor of Play* (2005) is worth rereading.

The psychoanalyst Neville Symington (Symington 1993) reminds us that there are subtler forms of nurturance failure that also have a profound impact on our capacity for empathy. Neville is a world expert on the narcissistic process, which he understands as a state of mind that always prefers fantasy and rejects the real. This is familiar to all of us as the 'morning after' syndrome. Here is an illustrative vignette.

Samantha and Brad Pitt's Clone

Here is little story from one of my patients, Samantha.

I was at a party with friends when Brad Pitt's clone came into my life across the proverbial crowded room. We exchanged phone numbers and went out on a date a couple of days later.

But Brad's name turned out to be Brian; he came from Gundagai and wore purple underpants. The following morning, I dismissed him. He just did not measure up to my original fantasy. And yet, I discovered later, when he began dating a girlfriend of mine, that he was a jazz pianist and loved dogs and children.

I realised that had I not been so fixated on the romantic vision and got to know the real being better, I may have even found that my opinion of purple underpants might have improved.

There is a tension between the fantasied and real, and narcissism is an unwillingness to engage with the *real*.

This dismissive approach to the real and actual has some of its roots in early nurturance patterns. When the parent's way of relating to the child is too appearance and performance-focused, the child internalises this and strives to be a pretty ballerina at the expense of her inner life. Thus she sees the world and herself through the 'performance' glasses, dismissing the real in favour of the cultivated performance.

Hannibal Lecter and Perspectival/Cognitive Empathy

Just as nurturance has its subtleties, so does empathy, this much misunderstood function. Empathy is not just the ability to read others' minds accurately. US child psychiatrist Bruce Perry (who looked after the children who survived the David Koresh cult disaster in Waco, Texas) has written several books that we recommend, including Szalavitz and Perry's *Born for Love: Why Empathy is Essential and Endangered* (2010). Perry uses the term *perspectival* to refer to the aspect of empathy that has to do with the ability to read someone else's mind accurately. The term *cognitive empathy* refers to the same function, and is used by researchers like Simon Baron-Cohen, professor of developmental psychopathology at the University of Cambridge in the United Kingdom (2011).

The murderous Hannibal Lecter of the book and movie *The Silence of the Lambs* (Harris 2002) is a great mind reader, all the better to eat you.

And the advertising industry employs some of the most sophisticated motivational psychologists / neuroscientists on the planet, all the better to sell you things. They are all very good with cognitive/perspectival maps of the other but devoid of *emotional* empathy, of impulses to feel for the other's benefit.

On the other hand, empathy cannot exist without cognitive maps. The autism sufferer struggles to get a cognitive map of where the other comes from but is tormented by strong and bewildering feelings, and defaults into ritualism to manage the turmoil, much as do some of our bureaucracies. In passing, we should say that autistic spectrum disorder is a condition which is, to the best of our understanding thus far, caused by a combination of genetic and biochemical factors. The quality of the microbiome, the gut bacteria, may contribute in some cases, for example, as can perinatal infection and toxins (Sajdel-Sulkowska 2013). But poor nurturance will contribute to worsening the condition, as it does for much else.

Empathy is also different from sympathy, which always patronises. Empathy is not sentimentality, which stays locked in the subject's revelling in their own feelings without a moment's consideration for the actual experience of the other. Sentimentality does not grant equal psychological status to subject and object. We could say that empathy is not only cognitive and affective but intersubjective in a very egalitarian way. The most empathic people I know are beings with a quietly electric sense of presence, the Dalai Lamas of this world. You really know they're fully there, with you, and with themselves.

Domestic Violence

Domestic violence is an especially dangerous form of abuse. And abuse comes in many forms. There is the violent lashing out that we see in people with poor impulse control. And we know that poor impulse control is a consequence of early abuse.

But there is also the cruelty and exploitation that we see in psychopathy and sociopathy. This may not necessarily involve physical violence but can have disastrous consequences nevertheless. However, the matter is further complicated by the fact that psychopathy seems to have a genetic basis, as we mentioned earlier. However, as we also mentioned earlier, studies by Dadds and others (Dadds et al, 2012, Fallon 2013) show that a child with a genetic loading for psychopathy can be helped with eye contact, mindfulness, and empathy therapies/ practices. By and large, families of children with psychopathic behavioural issues *'tend to be pretty good parents: motivated, engaged and loving, not high rates of abuse . . . The evidence so far is this is not something we can blame on the parents'* as Dadds says (2011). But if the nurturer is dysfunctional, they will not be able to implement various treatment programmes and may make the psychopathic child's impulse control even worse.

We have also mentioned earlier how the attachment dysfunctions that are a result of poor early nurturance skew our choice of partners quite unconsciously, and damaged women tend to end up with abusive partners.

There are, of course, some conditions, like schizophrenia, which can contribute to domestic violence. But even there, we know that early childhood abuse significantly increases the risk of developing schizophrenia.

However, irrespective of whether the perpetrator of domestic violence came from a background of poor impulse control, psychopathy, or psychosis, the problem remains. It is awful for the partner but also for the children and heightens the risk of transgenerational transmission.

A Fractal View of Nurturance

Empathy and mindfulness facilitate impulse control and make for both kindness and good limit setting. A range of interventions (meditation, psychotherapy) can boost these, but they involve much hard work, essentially because of our ingrained resistances, which have much to do with the core unsatisfactoriness of human existence (the Buddhist First Noble Truth). If it were easier, we would all Dalai Lamas. However, a good start in life helps a lot. As I have said so often before in this book, developmental neuroscience tells us that 'good enough' early nurturance makes for more mindful and compassionate beings. Babies and children find it hard enough to begin this developmental work, even with good nurturers. But various forms of nurturance failure and reactive attachment disorders, make things so much more difficult. Many of our interventions, no matter how well meaning, no matter how necessary, thus come too late.

But one of the lovely things about empathy is that it has a reverberating effect, a fractal 'similarity across scale' property.

We recently treated a severely abused young indigenous woman who was pregnant. Chapter 4 tells the full story. A 'reflective listening' engagement helped her develop a useful therapeutic alliance and allowed us in turn to extend this to interactions between her and her newborn baby girl. The successful bonding, in turn, gave the mother further vicarious repair. We ourselves received support from regular video links with a tertiary perinatal service. This spread across the various members of the team—midwives, obstetrician, postnatal workers, mental health workers—who could thus 'sing from the same page' in their empathic care of the mother and baby. The mother stopped drinking and using cannabis early on. Her mother, who had a severe drink problem, also gave up (without *any* prompting on our part) so as to be a better supporter for her daughter and granddaughter. The relatives who used to come to the house and get drunk and violent also moderated themselves, again, without *any* prompting. Fractal patterns everywhere. Now if *only* this could spread further: our politicians perhaps?

The whole point is, *if we could only get in earlier* and protect and nurture the mothers, we would spare each generation from the dreadful consequences.

Overview

We have looked at some of the core memes which underpin our present cultural world. And one of them is the developmental or early nurturance meme, the meme that Wati Kanyilpai exemplifies. In this chapter, we have looked at studies of how attachment patterns develop and what recent advances in brain imaging and other neurobiological investigations tell us about how the baby develops (or fails to develop) secure attachment dynamics. This secure basis makes possible an adequate capacity for empathy, mindfulness, and impulse control (a capacity for autonomy which is distinct from impulsiveness). Much of this depends on adequate early nurturance. And the advances over the last forty years or so in our understanding of this process can now guide us in developing ways of nurturing the nurturers more adequately. Despite good nurturance, some of us will still have problems, but overall, fewer of us will be severely affected.

And now, Wati Kanyilpai thanks deeply, from the bottom of his heart, all the neuroscientists and clinicians, the Bowlbys, Siegels, Schores, Teichers, Ainsworths, Fishers . . . (the list is huge) of this world for all their loving work in this vital field. He also extends his loving gratitude and encouragement to all of you who are extending these awarenesses in to the everyday world, the tender nurturance of the women and babies in those vital first three years of life.

BIBLIOGRAPHY

1. Ainsworth, M. D. S., and Wittig, B. A. (1969). 'Attachment and the Exploratory Behaviour of One-Year-Olds in a Strange Situation'. In B. M. Foss (Ed.), *Determinants of Infant Behaviour* Vol. 4, pp. 113–136. London: Methuen.

2. Ashley, A. (2016). Post to the Guardian on http://www.theguardian.com/science/2016/jan/12/whether-to-pick-sides-in-psychology-today.

3. Baron-Cohen, S. (2011). *Zero Degrees of Empathy: A New Theory of Human Cruelty.* Penguin UK. ISBN 9780713997910.

4. Bernier, A., and Meins, E. (2008). 'A Threshold Approach to Understanding the Origins of Attachment Disorganization'. *Developmental Psychology,* 44(4), 969–982.

5. Bowlby, R., King, P. (2004). *Fifty Years of Attachment Theory: Recollections of Donald Winnicott and John Bowlby.* Karnac Books. p. 17. *ISBN 9781855753853.*

6. Carlson, E. A. (1998). 'A Prospective Longitudinal Study of Attachment Disorganization/Disorientation'. *Child Development,* 69(4), 1107–1128.

7. Dadds, M. R., Allen, J. L., Oliver, B. R., Faulkner, N., Legge, K., Moul, C., Woolgar, M., Scott, S. (2012). 'Love, Eye Contact, and the Developmental Origins of Empathy v. Psychopathy'. *The British Journal of Psychiatry,* March 2012, 200 (3) 191–196; DOI: 10.1192/bjp.bp.110.085720.

8. Dadds, M. (2011) 'Bad to the Bone' (interview). *Sydney Morning Herald*. http://www.smh.com.au/national/bad-to-the-bone-20110919-1khts.html.

9. De Oliveira, C. A., Bailey, H. N., Moran, G., and Pederson, D. R. (2004). 'Emotion Socialization as a Framework for Understanding the Development of Disorganized Attachment'. *Social Development*, 13(3) 437–467.

10. Dubovsky, S. (2015). 'Does a Mother's Depression Affect Her Baby's Brain?' *Biol Psychiatry*.

11. Duschinsky, R. (2015). 'The Emergence of the Disorganized/ Disoriented (D) Attachment Classification, 1979–1982'. *History of Psychology* 18(1): 32–46.

12. Fallon, J. (2013). The Psychopath Inside: A Neuroscientist's Personal Journey into the Dark Side of the Brain. Penguin Group USA LLC New York 2013.

13. Fang X, Brown, D. S., Florence, C. S., Mercy, J. A.(2012). 'The Economic Burden of Child Maltreatment in the United States and Implications for Prevention'. *Child Abuse Negl*. Feb. 36(2):156–65. doi: 10.1016/j.chiabu.2011.10.006.

14. Fearon, R. P., Bakermans-Kranenburg M. J., van Ijzendoorn, M. H., Lapsley, A., and Roisman, G. I. (2010). 'The Significance of Insecure Attachment and Disorganization in the Development of Children's Externalizing Behaviour: A Meta-analytic Study', *Child Development*, 81(2), 435–456.

15. Felitti, V. J., Anda, R. F., et al. (May 1998). 'Relationship of Childhood Abuse and Household Dysfunction to Many

of the Leading Causes of Death in Adults: The Adverse Childhood Experiences (ACE) Study'. *American Journal of Preventive Medicine.* **14** (4): 245–258. doi:10.1016/S0749-3797(98)00017-8. PMID 9635069.

16. Fisher, S. (2014). *Neurofeedback in the Treatment of Developmental Trauma: Calming the Fear-Driven Brain.* Norton. NY.

17. Frewen, P., Lanius, R. (2015). *Healing the Traumatized Self: Consciousness, Neuroscience, Treatment.* WW Norton and Co.

18. Gyllenhaal, K. (2015). https://kindredmedia.org/2015/06/an-interview-with-in-utero-filmmaker-kathleen-gyllenhaal-includes-podcast-and-transcript/.

19. Harris, T., (2002). *The Silence of the Lambs.* Arrow.

20. Hrdy S. (2009). *Mothers and Others: The Evolutionary Origins of Mutual Understanding.* Cambridge: Harvard University Press. ISBN 0-674-03299-3.

21. Lanius, R., Vermetten, E., Pain, C., editors (2010). *The Impact of Early Life Trauma on Health and Disease: The Hidden Epidemic.* Cambridge University Press 2010.

22. Linden, D. J. (2015). *Touch: The Science of Hand, Heart, and Mind.* Penguin Books. Random House N.Y. ISBN 978-0-670-01487-3.

23. LSAC (The Longitudinal Study of Australian Children) (2013). *Growing Up in Australia: 2011–12 Annual Report.* Commonwealth of Australia. ISSN 1836-4314. ISBN 9781925007329

24. Lyons-Ruth, K. (2007). 'The Interface between Attachment and Intersubjectivity: Perspective from the Longitudinal Study of Disorganized Attachment', *Psychoanalytic Inquiry*, 26(4), 595–616;

25. Lyons-Ruth, K., and Jacobvitz, D. (2008). 'Attachment Disorganization: Genetic Factors, Parenting Contexts, and Developmental Transformation from Infancy to Adulthood'. In J. Cassidy and P. R. Shaver (Eds.), *Handbook of Attachment: Theory, Research, and Clinical Applications* (2nd ed., pp.666–697). New York: McGraw-Hill.

26. Lyons-Ruth, K., Bureau J.-F., Easterbrooks, M., Obsuth, I., Hennighausen, K., and Vulliez-Coady, L. (2013). 'Parsing the construct of maternal insensitivity: distinct longitudinal pathways associated with early maternal withdrawal', *Attachment and Human Development*, 15(5-6), 562–582.

27. MacDonald, H. Z., Beeghly, M., Grant-Knight, W., Augustyn, M., Woods, R. W., Cabral, H., Rose-Jacobs, R., Saxe, G. N., and Frank, D. A. (2008). 'Longitudinal Association between Infant Disorganized Attachment and Childhood Posttraumatic Stress Symptoms', *Development and Psychopathology*, 20(2), 493–508.

28. Main, M., and Cassidy, J. (1988). 'Categories of Response to Reunion with the Parent at Age 6: Predictable from Infant Attachment Classifications and Stable over a One-Month Period', *Developmental Psychology*, 24(3), 415–426.

29. Main, M., Hesse, E., Kaplan, N. (2005). 'Predictability of Attachment Behaviour and Representational Processes at 1, 6, and 18 Years of Age: The Berkeley Longitudinal

Study'. Grossman, K. E., Grossman, K., Waters, E. (Eds). *Attachment from Infancy to Adulthood.* Pp. 245–304. New York. Guilford Press. http://attachmentdisorderhealing. com/adult-attachment-interview-aai-mary-main/.

30. Main, M., and Solomon, J. (1990). 'Procedures for Identifying Infants as Disorganized/Disoriented during the Ainsworth Strange Situation'. In M. T. Greenberg, D. Cicchetti, and E. M. Cummings (Eds.), *Attachment In the Preschool Years: Theory, Research and Intervention* (pp. 121–160). Chicago: University of Chicago Press.

31. Main, M., and Solomon, J. (1986). 'Discovery of a New, Insecure-Disorganized/Disoriented Attachment Pattern'. In M. Yogman and T. B. Brazelton (Eds.), *Affective Development in Infancy* (pp. 95–124). Norwood, NJ: Ablex.

32. Meares, R. (2005). *The Metaphor of Play.* 3rd Edition. Routledge.

33. Mikulincer, M., and Shaver, P. R., (2007). *Attachment in Adulthood: Structure, Dynamics, and Change.* Guilford Press, New York.

34. Moss, E., Cyr, C., and Dubois-Comtois, K. (2004). 'Attachment at Early School Age and Developmental Risk: Examining Family Contexts and Behavior Problems of Controlling-Caregiving, Controlling-Punitive, and Behaviorally Disorganized Children', *Developmental Psychology*, 40(4), 519.

35. National Institute for the Clinical Application of Behavioral Medicine. http://www.nicabm.com/trauma-the-neurobiology-of-attachment-and-trauma/.

36. Nowak, M. (2001). *Supercooperators: Altruism, Evolution, and Why We Need Each Other to Succeed*. Free Press (The): New York, NY, 2011. ISBN 9781439100189.

37. Ogawa, J. R., Sroufe, L. A., Weinfield, N. S., Carlson, E. A., and Egeland, B. (1997). 'Development and the Fragmented Self: Longitudinal Study of Dissociative Symptomatology in a Nonclinical Sample', *Development and Psychopathology*, 9(4), 855–879.

38. Pettigrew, J., Miller, S. M., (1998). 'A "Sticky" Interhemispheric Switch in Bipolar Disorder?' *Proc. R. Soc. Lond. B* (1998) 265, 2141^2148 2141 & 1998. The Royal Society.

39. Pettigrew, J. (1998). http://www.uq.edu.au/nuq/jack/jack.html.

40. Pettigrew, J. (1998). http://www.uq.edu.au/nuq/jack/BipolarDisorder.html.

41. Petchkovsky, L., Petchkovsky, M., Dickson, P., Morris, P., Montgomery, D. Dwyer, J., Burnett, P., Strudwick, M. (2013). 'fMRI Responses to Jung's Word Association Test: Implications for Theory, Treatment and Research'. *The Journal of Analytical Psychology* 58(3):409–31.

42. Petchkovsky, L., Robertson-Gillam, K., Kropotov, J., Petchkovsky, M. (2013). 'Using QEEG Parameters (Asymmetry, Coherence, and P3a Novelty Response) to Track Improvement in Depression after Choir Therapy'. *Advances in Mental Health*, 11 3: 257–267. doi:10.5172/jamh.2013.11.3.257.

43. Sajdel-Sulkowska, E. M., Zabielski, R. (2013). 'Gut Microbiome and Brain-Gut Axis in Autism—Aberrant Development of Gut-Brain Communication and Reward Circuitry: Chapter 4; Mental and Behavioural Disorders and Diseases of the Nervous System'. In *Recent Advances in Autism Spectrum Disorders, Volume I.* Edited by Fitzgerald, M., ISBN 978-953-51-1021-7.

44. Sammut, J. (2015). *The Madness of Australian Child Protection.* Connorcourt Publishing 2015.

45. Sanson, A., Nicholson, J., Ungerer, J., Zubrick, S., Wilson, K., Ainley, J., Berthelsen, D., Bittman, M., Broom, D., Harrison, L., Rodgers, B., Sawyer, M., Silburn, S., Strazdins, L., Vimpani, G., Wake, M. (2002). *Introducing the Longitudinal Study of Australian Children.* Australian Institute of Family Studies—Commonwealth of Australia. ISBN 0 642 39496 2; ISSN 1447-1558 (Print); ISSN 1447-1566 (Online).

46. Schore, A. (2003). *Affect Dysregulation and Disorders of the Self.* WW Norton & Company.

47. Schore, A. (2012). *The Science of the Art of Psychotherapy.* WW Norton & Company. ISBN 978-0393706642.

48. Schore, A. 'Modern Attachment Theory: The Central Role of Affect Regulation in Development and Treatment'. *Clinical Social Work Journal*, 2008; 36: 9–20. DOI 10.1007/s10615-007-0111-7.

49. Siegel, D. (2011). *Mindsight: The New Science of Personal Transformation.* Bantam Book, New York. ISBN 978-0-553-38639-4.

50. Solomon, J., and George, C. (2011). 'The Disorganized Attachment-Caregiving System'. In Judith Solomon and Carol George (Eds.), *Disorganized Attachment & Caregiving*, pp. 25–51, NY: Guilford Press.

51. Sroufe, L. A., Carlson, E. A., Levy, A. K., and Egeland, B. (1999). 'Implications of Attachment Theory for Developmental Psychopathology', *Development and Psychopathology*, 11, 1–13.

52. Sroufe, L. A., Siegel, D. (2011). 'The Verdict Is In: The Case for Attachment Theory'. *Psychotherapy Networker*. Vol 35, No. 2. March/April.

53. Symington, N., (1993) *Narcissism: A New Theory*. Karnac Books.

54. Szalavitz, M., Perry, B. D. (2010). *Born for Love: Why Empathy is Essential and Endangered*. HARPER. ISBN 978-0-06-165679-8.

55. Van der Kolk, B. (2014). *The Body Keeps the Score*. Viking: ISBN10 0670785938 ISBN13 9780670785933.

56. Van der Kolk, B. (2005). 'Developmental Trauma Disorder: Toward a Rational Diagnosis for Children with Complex Trauma Histories,' *Psychiatric Annals* 35:5, 401-408, May. www.traumacenter.org/products/pdf_files/preprint_dev_trauma_disorder.pdf.

57. Van der Kolk, B. A., Pynoos, R. T. S., Ciccetti, D., Cloitre, M., D'Andrea, W., Ford, J. D., Lieberman, A. F., Putnam, F. W., Saxe, G., Spinazzola, J., Stolbach, B. C., Teicher, M.

(2009). *Proposal to Include a Developmental Trauma Disorder Diagnosis for Children and Adolescents in DSM-V. www. traumacenter.org/announcements/DTD_papers_Oct_09.pdf.*

58. Van Ijzendoorn, M. H., Schuengel, C., and Bakermans-Kranenburg, M. J. (1999). 'Disorganized Attachment in Early Childhood: Meta-analysis of Precursors, Concomitants, and Sequelae', *Development and Psychopathology*, 11, 225–249.

59. Teicher, M. H., Samson, J. A., Sheu, Y. S., Polcari, A., and McGreenery, C. E. (2010). 'Hurtful Words: Association of Exposure to Peer Verbal Abuse with Elevated Psychiatric Symptom Scores and Corpus Callosum Abnormalities'. *Am. J. Psychiatry.* 167(12):1464–71. doi: 10.1176/appi. ajp.2010.10010030.

60. Teicher, M. H., and Parigger, A. (2015). 'The "Maltreatment and Abuse Chronology of Exposure" (MACE) Scale for the Retrospective Assessment of Abuse and Neglect during Development'. *PLoS ONE*, 10(2): e0117423. doi:10.1371/journal.pone.0117423. http://journals.plos.org/plosone/article?id=10.1371/journal.pone.0117423.

61. Teicher, M. H., Samson, J. A., Anderson, C. M., Ohashi, K. (2016). 'The Effects of Childhood Maltreatment on Brain Structure, Function, and Connectivity'. *Nat. Rev. Neurosci.* 17(10):652–66. doi: 10.1038/nrn.2016.111.

62. Wilson, S., van der Kolk, B., Burbridge, J., Kradin, R., Fisler, R. (1999). 'Phenotype of Blood Lymphocytes in PTSD Suggests Chronic Immune Activation'. *Psychosomatics* 40(3):222–5, DOI: 10.1016/S0033-3182(99)71238-7

CHAPTER 4

Healing Trans-generational Cascades of Trauma and Distress in Disadvantaged Australian Indigenous Communities

Time to visit Wati Kanyilpai's home in Central Australia and see what is happening there.

This chapter is the core of our book. It describes the cascades of trauma seen in the remote indigenous communities we have been servicing for many years and the conditions that led to this. It also looks at how some healing could take place and describes some of the organisations that are beginning to offer real help.

And what we find there, the causes of the trauma and the ways we can fix it up, extends to the whole world. It extends to *you* dear reader.

Let us start with how my involvement first began.

The Rat Story

A couple of years after graduating in medicine and doing my obligatory hospital placements, I managed to get a very junior research placement at the Brain Research Unit at Callan

Park Mental Hospital in Sydney. The head of the unit—let's call him Professor Tocsin—had an international reputation for amphetamine research. My job was to assist his underling, Dr Robert Kirkby, a research neuropsychologist working with the effects of amphetamine on rats in the animal laboratory. There was a brilliant technician in the lab who had manufactured a tiny stereotactic frame with microelectrodes that we could place in neurones in the rats' caudate nuclei, to see what happened when they were on amphetamines, all the better to understand what might be happening in humans. We also noticed that when rats were high on amphetamines, they showed very typical stereotypical behaviours, clinging to the walls of the mazes, pacing back and forth, and making repetitive movements.

When a cohort of rats had finished an experiment, they usually got killed (or at least that was the enforced practice in those days). I felt very sorry for them, and several of them ended up in my home as pets (they make *great* pets). But I couldn't rescue them all. It seemed such a pity to waste them, and Rob and I decided that, if we couldn't save them, we might at least make some use of their poor bodies. We devised an experiment in which we homogenised the brains of some dead rats that had been in the amphetamine experiments and extracted a short polypeptide fraction which we then injected into naive rats. There was NO amphetamine in the extract, and yet, the recipients showed all the stereotypic behaviours seen in rats on amphetamines. Somehow, the polypeptide fraction had transferred amphetamine behaviour!

We submitted our findings to a rather controversial magazine of the time, then somehow, Professor Tocsin got to find out. He was incensed. We had used his rats without his permission! We had published a highly controversial paper in a highly controversial journal (Petchkovsky et al. 1975)! We had thereby tarnished the reputation of the Brain Research Unit! And *HE* was not included in the authorship list!

As the most junior member of the team, my head was on the chopping block, and I was summarily guillotined.

Unemployed, without any good references, I barely survived doing casual GP locums. But I noticed an advertisement for an interesting placement at Alice Springs Hospital in Central Australia, applied for it, and found myself working as an obstetrics and surgical registrar, delivering babies and removing appendices for the next two years, 1969 and 1970. It was there that I had my first contacts with indigenous people. It must have been infectious, because I've found myself returning to the Red Centre ever since.

Thirty Years of Involvement with Disadvantaged Indigenous Communities in Central Australia

In late 1970, I got a job at the University Department of Psychiatry in Manchester as a junior trainee, a psychiatric registrar. Training in child and adolescent psychiatry in Hampshire followed, as did a Jungian training analysis in London.

When I returned to Australia in 1975, I renewed my connection with Central Australia, visiting regularly, and working there full-time from 1992 to 1997 and 2005 to 2007. I have made regular visits since (monthly at first, then every second month since 2010), servicing remote indigenous communities in the Pitjantjatjara/Yankutjajara, Pintubu, Loritja homelands (Mimili, Yulara, Ikuntji, Watyawanu, Papunya and Walunguru/Kintore communities). I gradually learned to speak Western Deserts dialects well enough to do psychological assessments, and I developed relationships with a group of ngangkari/traditional healer mentors, who taught me a lot about the culture. These included the late Andrew Spencer Japaljari, an extraordinary pioneer in the field who developed HALT (the Healthy Aboriginal Lifestyles Team) in the '70s, the first organisation to systematically use Aboriginal languages and iconography to deliver health education. (See http://www.alicespringsnews.com.au/2015/12/08/eagle-and-crow-andrew-spencer-japaljarri/.)

As I described in Chapter 1, it was with Andrew and a group of indigenous healers (ngangkari) that I got an experiential feel for indigenous healing practices. This included the Watikanyilpai story.

Sweeping Dispossessions

As I continued working in Central Australia, it gradually became clear to me that even when European contact tried to be well-meaning, it could still prove disastrous because cultures are such fragile ecosystems. Traditionally, the classificatory kinship system that underpins all indigenous Australian cultures prescribes a range of helpers/nurturers (*kanyintjarra*, in Western Deserts dialects), whose role is to support young mothers through the perinatal period, thus ensuring that the attachment dynamics and interactions that are at the heart of infant neurodevelopment proceeded optimally, but with one interesting difference: the indigenous sense of self developed into a more 'distributive' configuration than the Western one, with deep senses of connection to kin but also 'land'. A detailed discussion of indigenous sense of self and 'maps of subjectivity' is available in Petchkovsky et al. (2004).

From the very first, contact began to make an impact on the traditional classificatory kinship structure, and various alienations and dispossessions followed. There was much (documented) disregard of the traditional classificatory kinship structure by early missionaries, many of whom exhorted people to ignore classificatory marriage laws (and thereby commit classificatory incest), resulting in generations of children who no longer had a place in the traditional social structure, and became more vulnerable to a range of mental illnesses (Petchkovsky 1982). To this day, many of the marginal and dispossessed people who live rough and sleep under bridges in Alice Springs are the products of culturally 'irregular' unions—people who no longer fit into their traditional society.

The Stolen Generations epoch in Australia is another example of gross failures of nurturance. Children (usually children of mixed Aboriginal/European parentage) were taken away from their Aboriginal families, their primary attachment objects, in order to supposedly protect them, but many of the new 'carers' proved negligent and harmful (Petchkovsky 2004).

There is a large literature base addressing a range of negative impacts on indigenous people. Some key publications would include Marmot on life expectancy (2005), Elliott-Farrelly on suicide rates (2004), John et al. on metabolic syndrome and mental illness (2009), Walker and McDonald on the over-representation of indigenous people in custody in Australia (1995), Rickwood and Eckersley on trends in mental health problems for indigenous youth and adolescents (2007), and Judy Atkinson (2002).

Emeritus Professor Judy Atkinson is a leading figure in the cultural trauma field. She has Jiman (Queensland) / Bundjalung (Northern NSW) ancestry. She has been doing reparative work for many years with disadvantaged indigenous communities across Australia and PNG. Her 2002 book *Trauma Trails: Recreating Songlines; The Transgenerational Effects of Trauma in*

Indigenous Australia provides context to the life stories of people who have moved / been moved from their country in a process that has created trauma trails and the changes that can occur in the lives of people as they make connections with each other and share their stories of healing. As well as reviewing the familiar range of traumas and stressors, she adds a factor unique to many indigenous populations. She calls this *historical trauma*, and we quote her definition of it (Atkinson 2005).

> *[This] is a type of trauma transmitted across generations (that is, intergenerational trauma). It is defined as the subjective experiencing and remembering of events in the mind of an individual or the life of a community, passed from adults to children in cyclic processes as 'cumulative emotional and psychological wounding' [. . .]. Duran and Duran (1995) suggest that historical trauma can become normalised within a culture because it becomes embedded in the collective, cultural memory of a people and is passed on by the same mechanisms through which culture, generally, is transmitted.*

Judy also reminds us (Atkinson 2013) that indigenous children are 5.4 times as likely as non-indigenous children to experience a hospital separation for assault, 8 times as likely to be the subject of substantiated child abuse or neglect, and 15 times as likely to be under juvenile justice supervision (AIHW 2015).

Patriarchal Hegemony

Jacinta Nampijinpa Price, a Walpiri woman from Yendumu in Central Australia, reminds us that in addition to all of the above, indigenous Australian culture is and has always been deeply patriarchal. In precolonial days, this was relatively unproblematic because the intact culture has so many provisions for early childhood nurturance embedded in the classificatory kinship system, where every mother had a range of culturally prescribed and easily available helpers to ensure that the babies and infants would receive a good enough early nurturance experience. But with postcolonial deculturation and overarching stress, this support system began to fragment, with the disastrous consequences we will be describing. There are now many more males with developmental trauma disorders than there would have been in precolonial times. But now, they use cultural justifications for their dysfunctional activities. In a thoughtful and very courageous article in *Meanjin*, an Australian periodical, Jacinta reminds us that currently, in traditional communities in the Northern Territory, dysfunctional men use the deeply embedded patriarchal and kin-based system for their own purposes (Price 2018). It's now common for female relatives of even violent offenders to support them against the victim!

This is where Wati Kanyilpai can begin to bring in some help, by encouraging the men to modulate their attitudes and behaviours towards more empathic and nurturant ways of being towards women.

Transgenerational Cascades of Distress in Disadvantaged Indigenous Communities

By now, you will have read Chapter 3 on developmental neuroscience, and learnt that the massive negative impact of disturbed nurturance on the neurodevelopment of all mammals and human beings is beyond debate.

Disadvantaged communities are particularly vulnerable, and their most vulnerable members are young mothers and their babies and infants in the first three or so years of life.

How does this play out in indigenous Australia? We were particularly struck by the fact that suicide rates in these communities during 2001–2006 were five times greater than those in the Caucasian population of the NT. We wondered about the impact of chronic stress on the development of that prefrontally mediated interiority (capacity for reflective inner life) that authors like Fonagy (2004) associate with the ability to deal with extreme emotional states, and published a paper on the subject (Petchkovsky et al. 2007). In this, we argued that the suicide gestures seen in the communities could be read as expressions of social powerlessness and implicit pleas for the kind of nurturance that might facilitate development of a capacity for reflectiveness/mindfulness that might lessen impulsive, emotional acting out. In turn, a limited mindfulness coupled with high levels of stress (violence, alcohol and drug abuse, fragmented sociocultural frames) made the nurturance of babies and infants more problematic, despite best intentions. This seemed to be setting further generations up for similar distresses.

The developing individual's impaired capacity for an inner life may be repaired to some extent, in psychotherapy, by the application of an empathic reflective nurturance (Fonagy 2004). But what is required in a social tragedy of this magnitude goes way beyond the psychotherapist's rooms. The authors extend this model of therapeutic nurturance, as heuristic metaphor, to the notion of the larger Euro-Australian milieu as failed nurturer, initially with sociopolitical interventions, based on economic models, and with a particular focus on psychiatric and forensic services. Demonstrable awareness of the centrality

NURTURING THE NURTURERS; HEALING THE PLANET

of nurturing the nurturers (the vulnerable young mothers) is conspicuously missing in these interventions.

In an attempt to see how organisations might become more effective nurturers, we used a Leximancer 'concept analysis' of coroners' reports to explore organisational 'collective countertransference' (Petchkovsky et al. 2007). The Leximancer data suggested major slippages between collective intentions and outcomes, as we saw in the Stolen Generations outcomes, where probably more than half of the adoptees did not survive past the age of thirty (Petchkovsky and San Roque 2002), prompting a discussion of ways of enhancing the nurturing capacities in organisations/services (in this case, psychiatry and the law), but more widely, a Kanyini/nurturance project of repair was outlined, beginning to address how the young mothers might best be supported.

Failures of Interventions: Failures of Social/Emotional Intelligence Programmes

Despite decades of interventions, indigenous Australian people continue to have lower life expectancies and higher rates of disease. They are also massively over-represented in the prison population. Children continue to present with a range of learning difficulties that limit their life prospects.

The authors contend that the European community's failure to provide adequate support and repair rests largely in a failure of social intelligence, a lack of collective mindfulness and empathy, even when there are good intentions. There has been a systemic failure of deep engagement in Aboriginal culture, and many frankly 'autistoid' interventions seem based on the mindsets of the interventionists rather than the actual needs of the recipients. (Missionary urges to disregard classificatory marriage laws would be one of many examples).

On a recent visit to Central Australia, the senior author learned that a young Aboriginal patient had killed his wife, and this had generated much anguished public discussion, some of it fuelled by the new Country National Party NT government, abusing their Labour predecessors for not having provided sufficient police.

While there is no doubt that a highly visible police presence can reduce violence in an inflamed community, the problem of recurring violence has more fundamental roots. In essence, violence is a failure of empathy and impulse control. And empathy and impulse control have major developmental determinants. Common sense points to the centrality of the earliest interventions possible. What is missed is the core of the problem, (1) the way transgenerational distress is mediated by failures of nurturance, and (2) the central solution, nurturing the nurturers, providing safety and support for young mothers during pregnancy and those vital early postnatal years.

Even more broadly, attachment and nurturance issues tend to get ignored in the political domain, the media, and the wider community. The baby-kissing and primary school visits that politicians display is clearly posturing, because it is not accompanied by any real 'nurturing the nurturers' awareness at the policy level. Paid parental leave may be a step in the right direction, but a nuanced understanding of attachment and nurturance behaviours and their impact on the developmental processes is nowhere to be found. Perhaps, as Anne Manne, author of the acclaimed book *Motherhood: How Should We Care for Our Children?* (2015) put it to us: 'Maybe it's because many of these people have avoidant attachment styles themselves' (Manne, personal communication, 2012).

But even if we put effective nurturance programmes in place, we are not likely to see their full impact on the coming generations for 10–20 years (at least in ways that can be picked up by government statistics). It therefore makes it difficult for politicians with restricted 'next election' horizons to offer much support—much easier to blame the previous administration for 'not providing enough police'.

Furthermore, public discussions of nurturance invariably generate heated ripostes from ideologues of various persuasions claiming these are merely attempts to further blame already marginalised mothers, though one suspects much of this animus is driven by the damaged attachment dynamics of the discussants. Nurturance remains a highly sensitive subject.

We are in any way not minimising the range of various important health social political and economic interventions that are actually informed by a more advanced social intelligence. They are extremely important, but effective prenatal, perinatal, and early infant interventions also need to be in place as early as possible. Preventing a car crash in the first place is better than treating the end result, no matter how skilfully.

Failures of Empathy and Mindfulness at the Organisational Level

Organisations dealing with indigenous mothers and children need to incorporate empathy and mindfulness into their cultures, but the actual task rests upon the individuals who run such organisations, and we suspect that many of us who are drawn to this kind of work come from various degrees of developmental dysfunction ourselves. And many sectors of the indigenous population also suffer disproportionately from this. But to the extent that people with such a background receive good quality repair, this background can be an advantage because it makes them more sensitively attuned.

As we said before, good nurturance relies on well-developed empathy and mindfulness. And in the last decade or so, these functions have been addressed across such a wide range of domains (including psychotherapy, meditation, autism, sociopathy, and developmental neuropsychology, to name a few) that it is sometimes difficult to know quite what is being referred to when these functions are referenced. For our discussion purposes, a basic working definition would be, empathy is a kindly awareness of the inner processes (the subjectivity) of the *other*, and mindfulness is the accurate awareness of *one's own* inner processes. This is the sense in which these terms are used by researchers like Dan Siegel and his colleagues (2007).

How does an organisation dealing with indigenous issues **develop** an empathic culture? Being female is an advantage, because women's empathy circuits tend to be better developed than men's. Women working in this area can have a powerful positive influence. Many areas of the brain are involved: the mirror neuron sites (how we perceive others), the insula (how we experience ourselves), the cingulate gyrus and the medial prefrontal cortex (how we compare the two). Child psychiatrist Dan Siegel collectively calls these brain areas the 'resonance circuitry' (2011). As for the male workers, meditation (especially 'loving-kindness' meditation practices) and mindfulness practices could obviously help a lot.

Adverse Consequences in Central Australian Remote Communities: Some Prevalence Studies

The Central Australian Remote Communities currently serviced by the authors share the high rates of violence (including domestic violence), imprisonment, unemployment, metabolic syndrome disorders, and drug and alcohol abuse that are seen across many other disadvantaged indigenous communities. It is important to emphasise they are some of the most functional and progressive remote communities in Central Australia. There are many good-hearted people in them working hard to nurture the children. We suspect that many other remote communities may be even more troubled. Nevertheless, even in the more benign communities, babies reared in these environments are subjected to high levels of stress, as are their mothers and carers, who, as Alan Schore reminds us, may unwittingly transmit this to the infants' developing brains. The stressors include a breakdown of empathy / social skills / nurturance skills, as well as the broader factors of deculturation, social and economic disadvantage, and prevalent domestic violence and community violence.

How does this affect individuals, especially the men? I was recently filling in for a colleague in the psychiatric unit in Alice Springs Hospital in Central Australia. An intelligent but deeply dysfunctional young Aboriginal man had been brought into the hospital with a ferocious drug-fuelled psychosis and was being looked after in a locked part of the facility. After several days of violence, he began to settle somewhat, largely thanks to two excellent security officers (both of them originally from Nigeria). They would sit with him in the tiny locked courtyard and comfort him in a non-invasive way, listening to his grievances, and gently miming his body language in subtle but supportive ways, like rocking gently when he rocked more forcefully. I would sometimes sit in the courtyard with them and talk with the patient in one of the local Pitjantjatjara dialects. At one point, I grew overambitious. Knowing that he had a background of continuous severe sexual abuse throughout his early childhood, I said to him that his childhood was awful.

He rose to his feet, glared at me, and raised his fists to strike me. I realised in that moment that I had unwittingly 'shamed' him. He did not want these matters opened up in the presence of the security officers. This would make him feel *kunta* (the word for shame, one of the most difficult emotions a tribal man could feel). And so, I apologised in dialect, and he began to settle. But I could so easily have become yet another casualty of murderous rage. And I wished we could have been there when he was an infant, to protect and nurture him, so that he could grow into his potential with an easier heart. And we are the ones who should be feeling *kunta*/shame, for having failed him and thousands of others.

Here we will focus on three areas: suicide, FASD, and childhood mental disorders.

1. High Indigenous Suicide Rates in Central Australia

In Central Australia (Alice Springs and remote indigenous communities) suicide rates during 2001–2006 were some ten times greater than those in the Caucasian population (NT Police Statistics in Petchkovsky et al. 2007). The authors considered that the high chronic stress endured by the indigenous residents could have impacted badly on the development of prefrontally mediated interiority (capacity for reflective inner life) that researchers like Fonagy (2004) have associated with the ability to deal with extreme emotional states. Struggles with reflectivity and impulse control are two of the main features of developmental trauma disorder. Thus, the many suicide gestures seen in the communities could be understood as consequences of developmental trauma disorder, expressions of social powerlessness and implicit pleas for the kind of nurturance that might facilitate development of a capacity for reflectiveness/ mindfulness that might lessen impulsive emotional acting out.

2. High Prevalence of Foetal Alcohol Syndrome (FAS) / Foetal Alcohol Spectrum Disorder (FASD) in Central Australia

Many pregnant women in these disadvantaged communities are highly stressed. Some of them drink a lot of alcohol to soothe themselves. This has resulted in a high incidence of foetal alcohol syndrome in the babies. Rate of FAS/FASD in indigenous children in the Northern Territory is some six times higher than expected, between 1.87 and 4.7 cases per 100 live births (1.8–4.7 per cent) (Harris and Bucens 2003), as against between 2 and 7 cases per 1,000 live births (0.2–0.7 per cent) in the wider population. The Australian Institute of Health and Welfare 2015 provides a good overview of interventions for prevention and management of FAS in Indigenous communities. (Australian Institute of Health and Welfare 2015). Prevalence of FASD in the child population of Loritja Loop communities observed by the present authors is around 4 per cent as against 1.08 per cent in the overall Australian population (Roozen, Peters, et al. 2016).

3. High Prevalence of Psychiatric Distress in Children in the Loritja Loop Communities

Here are some case vignettes to illustrate some of the problems we encounter and some of the approaches that sometimes help.

Reactive Attachment Disorder

Tessa's mother had a severe alcohol problem, and Tessa was abused and neglected so severely that at the age of three months, she had to be removed by the Department of Family Services. She was eventually placed with foster carers who proved inadequate. She was four when her grandmother Wendy, an indigenous Health Worker, took over as her primary carer, but by that time, she had sustained severe developmental damage and was very difficult to look after, despite all of Wendy's skills and caring.

Tessa's presenting complaints and symptoms cover a wide range. The most significant feature is that there are times when she gets violent, enraged, and impossible to control. These episodes go on for a long time and often result in her acting out in various awful ways, including killing animals and throwing sharp objects around. Her academic progress is also poor even though she is quite bright. There are attention and concentration difficulties, poor impulse control, and learning problems.

Her attachment behaviours are the sort of thing that we see in a reactive attachment disorder. It takes a long time for her to develop any bonding with nurturing adults, and even when she has developed some sort of bond, she is often inconsolable when she has one of her severe temper and violence outbursts. She is frequently unapproachable, even by her closest carer, Wendy. At those times, Tessa rejects any attempt at giving comfort by her carers. This is also true of the school situation, where she has formed some good bonds with some of the workers but again display the kind of attachment behaviours that are described as disorganised, avoidant, and anxious.

On psychological examination, she was reserved but interacted with me. Her eye contact was good. She was not fidgety at the time. She did, however, at the end of the interview, refuse to go back to the classroom and walked off to the shop.

Physical examination showed some signs that could be consistent with some foetal alcohol syndrome features. Her head is small. She had a thin upper lip, but her nasal philtrum seemed more or less within normal limits.

There is a range of vectors here which include some foetal alcohol syndrome symptomatology and some features of attention deficit and impulse control disorder, but the overwhelming vector that would account for her extreme behaviours would be reactive attachment disorder. She lives in a state of chronically high brain alert and is unable to derive sufficient comfort from carers.

In a well-resourced environment, children like Tessa would get intensive and prolonged psychotherapy. This would be combined with neurofeedback to reduce the high levels of brain arousal, and a range of mindfulness and empathy training exercises would also be employed to help the process along.

Intensive psychotherapy and neurofeedback are not available. On the positive side, she does have a very good carer and some excellent teachers and teacher's aides at school. This has helped with some healing of her process. Over the next period, we will prepare some protocols and learning resources for the staff so that they can continue to develop their management skills for Tessa's condition and for similar problems that they encounter in some of their other pupils.

FASD

Andrew Whistler is a likeable twelve-year-old boy. We first saw him when he was six. His mother drank heavily during her pregnancy and was a poor nurturer.

Ambrose has the classical FASD sentinel facial features: short palpebral fissure, smooth philtrum, thin upper lip.

He has a learning disorder and attention, concentration, and impulse-control problems. Nevertheless, he was eventually fostered out to a more nurturing family who lived in a more accepting community, and he got a lot of support from some of the local children, who engaged him in football, which he enjoyed. He also had a very supportive teacher.

He has done very well, but more recently, we learned from his teacher that because Andrew is now twelve, he has been moved into a high school curriculum class. Because of the cognitive problems that come with FASD and a certain amount of developmental trauma disorder, he is finding this very challenging. We are currently supporting his teacher in deploying a stress management protocol for him.

Clearly, most of the children with FASD will also have some degree of developmental trauma disorder, some of it amounting to reactive attachment disorder. ADHD will also be a feature of their symptomatology.

Conduct Disorder

Stuart is now twelve. He was first seen by us when he was 6. He was very large for his age and tended to use his size to bully other children. This included involving other children in killing animals, like young calves, by stabbing them and cutting their throats! A visiting paediatrician felt psychiatric and psychological reviews were indicated.

His family of origin was very dysfunctional, and he was eventually looked after by his uncle and aunt. Clearly, some degree of developmental trauma disorder has played a role in his overall pathology.

One of his teachers had some formal empathy and mindfulness training, and we combined this with the Mark Dadds 'eye contact' protocols. (Dadds 2012).

Stuart made remarkable progress over the next two years and is now much more settled. He is more caring with other children, and there have been no further episodes of cruelty to animals.

ADHD

William Johnson is an eleven-year-old boy with ADHD and mild foetal alcohol syndrome who was first seen in March 2013 when he was seven. There may also have been a developmental trauma component his presentation because his parents were dysfunctional. But he was being cared for by Lorna Johnson, his classificatory grandmother, who is a good carer.

The visiting paediatrician also thought that William had ADHD and wanted to start him on Ritalin. Feedback from the teachers confirmed that this diagnosis had some merit. William was definitely continuously restless and impulsive in the classroom and found it difficult to contain his various behaviours. His grandmother confirmed that is how William was at home as well, even to the extent with struggling to watch favourite TV programmes.

William also has some cognitive delays. At the social-emotional level, he seems to be aware of his oddness and prefers to stay with the group of children one year younger than him because they tolerate him more easily, and he finds himself more comfortable with them.

In May 2014, William had been on methylphenidate sustained release 18 mg daily for 6 months. The headmaster confirmed that William was doing very well on the Ritalin and his behaviour was much more manageable. The school also noted how, because over the weekends, times when methylphenidate is not taken, William's behaviour on the Mondays tended to be a bit more erratic until the methylphenidate finally kicked in. We explained that this was a downside that had to be tolerated because it was good for children on methylphenidate to take a regular break from it so they do not develop tolerance.

In November 2014, the teachers all reported that he continued to be less impulsive, more interactive and a better student. They are also very appreciative of the good nurturance that his grandmother Lorna was giving him. In March 2015, the visiting paediatrician felt his methylphenidate dose needed to be increased. He was placed on 27 mg of Concerta.

William's behaviour improved further. One of the significant components of this improvement is his love of music, and when we saw him, he was having a good time playing the guitar. His musical talents need to be encouraged.

The majority of the children seen in the remote communities we service will have some degree of developmental trauma disorder, given the stressful and challenging environments they grow in. It is therefore often difficult to tell if their attention deficits have a genetic or developmental basis. And FASD can also cause attention problems.

One mode of clarification is to observe how a child functions in the presence of a teacher they have formed a good attachment bond with. Typically, they can concentrate on their work so long as the teacher is giving them one-on-one attention. As soon as the teacher has to attend to someone else, concentration fails. For a child with a genetically based ADHD, whether the teacher is there may make little difference. It is of course possible for a child to have a genetic, a developmental, and a brain damage FASD component to their attention disorder.

Searching through our data files, we could not find a single child who could be categorised as having only ADHD without either FASD or DTD or both. The closest we could find is the case described above.

Given this complex aetiology, the ADHD neuromarkers found in quantitative EEG studies could help refine the diagnosis a little further. And the availability of neurofeedback protocols for ADHD could help with treatment. (Neurofeedback is on the American Academy of Paediatrics Evidence Base list of effective treatments for ADHD).

The brevity of our visits to the communities does not allow us to use QEEG and neurofeedback.

We therefore involve our paediatrician colleagues and sometimes do methylphenidate trials with children with ADHD symptoms, with occasional successes.

Prevalence Studies of Child Psychiatric and Psychological Disorders in Remote Disadvantaged and Indigenous Communities

What follows is Australia's first prevalence study on the subject. No other prevalence studies of child psychiatric disorders in disadvantaged Australian indigenous communities can be found in a literature search.

Indigenous child psychiatrist Professor Helen Milroy was appointed in February 2013 as a commissioner for the Royal Commission into Institutional Responses to Child Sexual Abuse. She and her colleagues collected a huge amount of important data on the subject, but when I spoke with her recently at the 2018 International Child Trauma Conference in Melbourne, she told me that thus far, no one yet had published a prevalence study on childhood psychological and psychiatric disorders in disadvantaged indigenous communities!

One publication, Stanley et al.'s *Child Abuse and Neglect in Indigenous Australian Communities* (2003) acknowledges that child distress is a major issue but lacks prevalence data and a developmental neurosciences perspective.

The mental health statistics of the children living in the Loritja Loop, as recorded in Central Australian Remote Mental Health Services documentation, were examined in March 2016. There were 251 children enrolled in the four schools. Walungurru School had 57 enrolled students, Papunya 130, Watiyawanu 42, and Ikuntji 22. The number of children on our remote mental health services active patient list was 52, some 20 per cent of the total. The diagnoses were all made to *DSM-5* criteria, except for developmental trauma disorder, where the van der Kolk criteria applied (Schmid et al. 2013), and sensory processing disorder (as per *DC:0–3R; Zero to Three* 2005 criteria). .

We have already mentioned that the prevalence of foetal alcohol spectrum disorder (FASD) among the children that we see in these communities is around 4 per cent. But there is also a range of other neurodevelopmentally mediated disorders with high prevalence. These include:

1. developmental trauma disorder (DTD), 26 children (10 per cent)
2. reactive attachment disorder (RAD), 15 children (6 per cent)
3. attention deficit hyperactivity disorder (ADHD). 21 children (8 per cent)
4. autistic spectrum disorder (ASD), 2 children (<1 per cent)
5. plus a range of as yet formally unquantified;
   - conduct disorders (CD)

- learning disabilities (LD)
- sensory processing disorders (SPD).

This last, sensory processing disorder, though not in *DSM-5*, is currently accepted in the <u>*Diagnostic Classification of Mental Health and Developmental Disorders of Infancy and Early Childhood*</u> (*DC:0-3R; Zero to Three* 2005). We mention it because our impression is that it may form a significant component of the case presentations.

Many of the children had multiple diagnoses (for instance, FASD and ADHD, DTD, CD, LD).

The authors of a British study on prevalence of RAD in a deprived British population (Minnis et al. 2013) calculated that in 1,646 children studied, there were 23 children with definite RAD diagnoses, suggesting that the prevalence of RAD in this population was 1.40 per cent (95 per cent, CI 0.94–2.10). Our Loritja Loop prevalence statistic for RAD to *DSM-5* criteria was 6 per cent, more than four times the British figure. These results are a cause for concern.

We remind the reader that given the relatively high functional level of the Loritja Loop communities, prevalence rates in other communities are likely to be even higher.

'I Feel I Have a Real Purpose Now': A Case Report to Illustrate What Can Be Done

A case report from the NSW Northern Rivers district (where I live when I am not travelling to the Northern Territory) illustrates some aspects of our earlier discussions and some of the principles of good 'nurturing the nurturers' practices and outcomes,

BC, an Aboriginal woman, thirty-three, from the Northern Rivers region in New South Wales, with a history of serial sexual abuse by males from infancy, had adopted an exclusively lesbian lifestyle. Her first-ever nonabusive heterosexual relationship, at the age of thirty-three, with a visitor from East Africa, resulted in a pregnancy. She had been abusing alcohol and cannabis heavily for years and had a history of psychiatric hospitalisations. Apart from the substance abuse, she had received a range of diagnoses including schizophrenia, schizoaffective disorder, drug-induced psychosis, borderline personality disorder, depression, and anxiety. She also had impulse control problems, with violent outbursts. Of further concern were her reports that at times she had thoughts of wanting to harm children.

She was living with her mother, who had a severe alcohol problem, and the household was constantly visited by violent alcohol- and drug-abusing relatives / extended relatives.

She came to our attention (and that of the Child and Family Services) when she was fourteen weeks pregnant. The prognosis was extremely bleak, with a high risk of foetal alcohol syndrome, post-partum depression or psychosis, and infant neglect and abuse. Initial interagency planning was to support her as best we could through the pregnancy and make arrangements to have the baby taken into care.

BC's psychiatric case manager was RJ, who saw her regularly, at least weekly, and developed a trusting therapeutic alliance with her. RJ referred her to LP for further support.

LP had worked with a range of Aboriginal communities for decades, which made for some level of cultural competence. He began seeing BC regularly, who, on this basis and with the help of RJ, found it easier to establish a therapeutic alliance with LP.

The State-wide Outreach Perinatal Service for Mental Health (SwOPS-MH) (swops@swahs.health.nsw.gov.au) is a pilot program based at Westmead Hospital, Sydney, to provide a consultation liaison service for perinatal mental health client, was engaged and provided fortnightly to monthly video link conferences with Professor Philip Boyce and colleagues (University of Sydney, Westmead Hospital). BC attended it regularly. A large benefit of the video link conferences was that the supportive nurturance by SwOPS-MH extended to the obstetrics and perinatal personnel, thus making it easier for all involved to develop a shared understanding and management procedures for this challenging case.

BC stopped drinking alcohol and gradually reduced her consumption of cannabis to optimise her baby's welfare. On initial presentation, she had been on Haloperidol. However, akathisia was making it difficult for her to sleep at night, and she was given chlorpromazine 50 mg nocte instead, and a small dose of risperidone (2 mg bd).

When the foetus began kicking in the womb, BC became anxious, worrying this meant the baby was distressed and did not like her. She gained considerable relief when an SSRI (sertraline 50 mg daily) was introduced and combined with some supportive psychotherapy.

Our interactions with BC focused on mindfulness and empathy. We used a lot of reflective listening with her so she could feel empathised with. This, in turn, made it easier for her to begin to develop more self-awareness and become more comfortable with preverbal vocalisations and gestures to prepare her for interactions with her baby. Prenatally, we mimed interactions with the baby for her, both towards it while it was in the womb and in post-partum fantasy to prepare her for the actual event.

Another important form of support was with material necessities. RJ and the MH Services helped BC negotiate agencies like Centrelink and procure a layette, stroller, bassinet, and various other baby-care requirements.

BC's mental state continued to improve through the pregnancy, and she had a normal labour. She was so well that we discontinued her risperidone. Although unable to breastfeed, she nevertheless proved adept at tuning in to her new born daughter's needs and received further unobtrusive coaching from us as we interacted with her while she interacted with her baby. The bonding process evolved warmly and positively.

In the meanwhile, BC's mother, without any prompting from us, had stopped drinking in order to provide her daughter with the best possible support. The extended family who used to visit her house and get drunk also moderated their behaviour so that when BC returned to her mother's house, the environment was much more supportive.

On her first video conference with SwOPS, BC had been so tense she was barely able to say anything. On her last video conference, one month postpartum, she spontaneously said to Professor Boyce, 'This has changed my life big time. I feel I have a real purpose now.'

BC developed iPhone skills to take photos of the baby and send them to her helpers. She enlarged a photo of RJ with the baby, framed it, and gave it to RJ as a token of her gratitude. In return, RJ took photos of BC interacting with her baby and gave them to BC (see Figure 1 below). RJ has given us written permission to include this picture in the publication because it shows so clearly the facial and bodily expressions of good attachment dynamics in a way that text cannot, and because she hopes this will inspire other mothers.

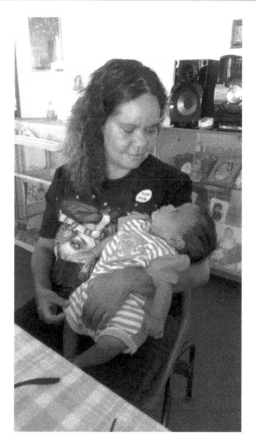

Figure 1

At the time of writing this chapter, BC's baby was two years old and thriving. BC has had one episode of drinking during all this time but made sure that her baby was well looked after and safe on that particular night.

There has been no symptomatology suggestive of post-partum depression or psychosis. The experience of receiving nurturing so that she can optimise her own nurturance, coupled with the vicarious repair she has received through being a good nurturer to her own baby, have had a very positive impact. We expect that there will inevitably be setbacks of one kind or another further down the track, but we also feel that the resilience she has developed through this process will enable her to ask for help appropriately and cope further.

And most importantly, BC's little daughter is getting a good neurodevelopmental start in life.

Helpful Organisations

Some of the more promising general interventionist approaches include the recommendations described by Richard Trugden in *Why Warriors Lie Down and Die* (2000), who recommend linguistic and cultural immersion for interventionists.

Noel Pearson is an Aboriginal Australian lawyer, academic, land rights activist and founder of the Cape York Institute for Policy and Leadership, an organisation promoting the economic and social development of Cape York (Pearson 2010). He brings high levels of social and political intelligence and a sophisticated insider's perspective to flawed interventionalism. He laments the disastrous intergenerational impact of mindless 'welfarism' and argues that organisations like Job Services Australia, who are purportedly supporting Aboriginal employment, actually have a self-serving dynamic. He has also been a strong supporter of the successful 'direct instruction' educational system being pioneered in Cape York to remedy the literacy and numeracy crisis in indigenous communities. As Nicholas Rothwell points out in a recent article on the subject (2014), the DI programme is highly interactive. The teaching model favours heuristic over prescriptive models of learning (developing capacities to generate paradigms, rather than being given prescriptive paradigms). Its positive results are enhanced by high empathic skills of the teachers, resonating with parents and children. This is combined with the social nurturance input of the Cape York

Aboriginal Australian Academy: 'The linchpin [is] the CYAAA' which provides 'two or three case managers . . . attached to each school [to support] high attendance'.

We have learned recently that the DI program has been discontinued for a variety of implausible reasons put forwards by government administrators. This is a tragedy and is yet another example of organisational blindness to nurturance issues.

The work of Pearson and colleagues with disadvantaged communities, when it has been allowed to progress, was transformative. Good education is vital for the next generation. The success of the DI programme was heartening, targeting a younger age range of recipients, with a higher level of neuroplasticity. Nevertheless, without effective and even earlier 'nurturing the nurturers' programmes in place, such interventions can still come too late, when the little recipients are already struggling with developmental damage.

Some other initiatives are closer to the early developmental mark.

Dr John Boulton is a paediatrician who has been working in Aboriginal communities for many years. Another article by Nicholas Rothwell in the *Weekend Australian* (Rothwell 2013) reviews some of this work. In essence, (quoting from Rothwell's article),

> 'if an unborn child is malnourished in the womb' . . . [but also if the mother is subject to high stress levels, and also if she overdoes alcohol and drugs because she feels so miserable] . . . 'blood is directed as the first priority to the brain, leaving the kidneys and other organs insufficiently developed . . . the child will grow up with a degree of insulin resistance' . . .

But also more broadly, there will be HPA axis dysfunction, with its consequent metabolic syndrome disorder. These are explained in detail in posts on our Politics of Nurturance (https://watikanyilpai.wordpress.com/) blog.

Rothwell continues.

> *'This in turn leads to early-onset diabetes . . . (and) the child will have a propensity to high blood pressure, heart disease, stroke and eventual kidney failure' . . . 'Key signs in young kids are a combination of poor growth plus a tendency to put fat on in the middle of the body.'*

But the psychological effects are also dreadful: ADHD, poor impulse control, chronic dysthymia (feeling miserable), learning difficulties, etc. . . . Again, I have detailed this in earlier Watikanyilpai blogs.

And to make matters even worse, many of the highly stressed pregnant women drank a lot of alcohol to soothe themselves. This has resulted in a high incidence of foetal alcohol syndrome in the babies. Rate of FAS in indigenous children in the Northern Territory is some 6 times higher than expected, between 1.87 and 4.7 cases per 1,000 live births (Harris and Bucens 2003), as against between 2 and 7 cases per 1,000 live births (0.2–0.7 per cent) in the wider population.

A good overview of the Australian situation is provided by Australian Institute of Health and Welfare 2015.

This problem is obviously not confined to indigenous communities, but given their already high level of stress, it adds even more of a burden.

Early nurturance of the nurturers is a recommended intervention, but this needs groups of people in various disadvantaged communities to set up suitable nurturance programmes, and this is not an easy task.

There are also some encouraging signs of early nurturance awareness in other quarters. Yeo and colleagues argue that 'the core hypotheses of attachment theory such as caregiver sensitivity, competence and secure base have to be based on the Australian Aboriginal people's cultural values' (Yeo 2003). Cargo and Warner (2013) a have performed a case study of the Aboriginal Parental Engagement Program (APEP) in South Australia to fine-tune it. Arney and colleagues, again in South Australia, look at a range of issues in working with Aboriginal families with young children. They describe the work of the Family Home Visiting Program in Metropolitan South Australia, which aims to build attachment between infants and parents (Arney et al. 2010). In Sydney, the twelve-week Boomerangs Parenting Program has developed to improve parenting skills and the parent–child relationship in indigenous families with young children (Lee et al. 2010).

On a broader level, our searches discovered that there is an organisation called Early Childhood Australia, which began in 1938 as the Australian Association of Pre-School Child Development, focusing on the very early years of childhood! It has been active in various ways over seventy-five years, offering a range of volunteer, activist, and advocacy services. Based in Canberra, Australia's capital city, it has branches in every state, including the Northern Territory, and has taken a strong interest in the welfare of indigenous children. And yet it clearly has a surprisingly low profile. It was only recently that I discovered, after decades of work with indigenous children, that it had a presence in the Northern Territory. I suspect its relative neglect is yet another symptom of the collective cultural avoidance of nurturance awareness. Details of ECA can be found on its website, http://www.earlychildhoodaustralia.org.au.

Bumps to Babes and Beyond: A Leading Initiative

The various programmes mentioned earlier have great merit. However, Australia's leading programme in this area is, in our view, the Babes to Bumps and Beyond initiative in the Mallee district of Victoria (Allen and Watson 2014). This is Australia's first-ever indigenous initiated 'nurturing the nurturers' programme. In conversation with co-founders Allen and Watson at the August 2014 Child Trauma Conference in Melbourne, we learned that this program was initiated and maintained by local Aboriginal communities and informed by the latest understanding of attachment theory and developmental neuroscience. The Bumps to Babes and Beyond initiative focusses on pregnant Aboriginal women aged fourteen to twenty-five and was introduced in 2012 by Mallee District Aboriginal Services (MDAS) with support from one of the leading parenting centres in Australia, the Victorian Queen Elizabeth Early Parenting Centre (QEC). It identifies young pregnant mothers at risk and offers empathic, culturally sensitive pre- and postnatal support for the first two to three years of the infant's life, helping mothers develop attuned and secure bonding with their children. It also offers pragmatic help for them in negotiations with Centrelink Child Support Services and the procurement of baby prerequisites like bassinets, prams, etc. A detailed evaluation of the program can be accessed in pdf form at **http://tinyurl.com/ndawafq**. We strongly recommend it to the reader. This is precisely what is needed nationally to begin the transgenerational healing process we support so strongly.

Bumps to Babes and Beyond presents a thoughtful and compassionate example for the nation and the world since dysfunctional early nurturance is a global problem and, arguably, the subjective/inner life equivalent of the climate crisis we all face. The only extra dimension I would add to Bumps and Babes is to include more *men* in the program and service delivery.

The Wirraka Maya Health Service Dreamtime Project

Even more recently, another perinatal indigenous nurturance programme has been established, this time in Western Australia: the Wirraka Maya Health Service Dreamtime Project (See Wirraka Maya 2015). Comments below are taken directly from their website. Beginning in August 2015, Port Hedland's Wirraka Maya Health Service will trial the Dreamtime Journey program with up to fifteen women in their first trimester of pregnancy, encouraging pregnant Aboriginal women in Western Australia's Pilbara to bond with their children while still in the womb to prevent neglect and abuse.

'Wirraka Maya chief executive June Councillor said a lot of families the service worked with were affected by child sexual abuse, alcohol, drugs and domestic violence. Staff had noticed new mothers were often not bonding with their children. In what is believed to be the first program of its kind, the women will be encouraged to read, sing and tell stories to their unborn children to forge a strong bond between them' . . . 'What we want to prevent is another wave of the Stolen Generation, where if the mum and bub isn't connected, there is that chance the baby could be neglected, Ms Councillor said. So what we want to try and do is prevent that because we are trying also to prevent our children going into care. We need to start now and need to start while the baby is still in the womb. If the mother and the baby [are] more strongly connected, when the baby is born, the mother is more likely to nurture the baby and to look after the baby and less likely to neglect the baby.'

We look with gratitude and admiration at the Bumps to Babes and Beyond and Wirraka Maya initiatives. They are so good that they can serve as models not just for other indigenous groups but for the wider community.

The Cross Borders Indigenous Family Violence Program for Men

Men have an important role in primary nurturance. There is a sense in which, in this domain, men are both part of the problem but also part of the solution. Women have always carried the primary burden of infant nurturance, while men have focused on being providers and protectors. But excesses can occur when providing and protecting are not coupled with empathy and a more fundamental understanding of nurturance. They can include greed and violence. We believe that one of the most central initiatives in a 'nurturing the nurturers' program is a positive input from men, aimed at reducing levels of domestic and community violence and providing empathic care and protection for the mothers and infants.

We recently learned on a visit to one of the remote communities (Ikuntji) of an extraordinary initiative called the Cross Borders Indigenous Family Violence Program. This small unit of 7.5 staff, operating since 2007, is administered by the Department for Correctional Services (South Australia) and is located in Alice Springs, Northern Territory. Cross Borders delivers a fifty-four-hour program that is specifically designed for perpetrators of family violence in the Ngaanyatjarra Pitjantjatjara Yankunytjatjara (NPY) Lands in remote Central

Australia. This area has a population of approximately 6,500 people spread over an area of 500,000 square kilometres across the Northern Territory, Western Australia, and South Australia. During the past eight years, seventy-one programs have been delivered, with over 420 men successfully completing the programs. This program is supported by the above state and territory governments as well as the Commonwealth government through the Department of Prime Minister and Cabinet.

Graeme Pearce commenced as the manager of Cross Border Programs on 12 January 2007. Referrals come to the organisation from the Corrective Services in three Australian states (the Northern Territory, South Australia, and Western Australia, hence 'Cross Borders'). As indigenous male prisoners prepare for discharge, one of their parole conditions can be to attend a fifteen-day impulse control and nurturance skills course in their community of residence. The workers involve Aboriginal elders in the program and have had very good results, increasing men's nurturance skills and reducing violence. A good account of this, called "Outline of Indigenous Family Violence Offender Program" (Holcombe and Willis 2015) can be found at http://tinyurl.com/hnp6syf .

We mentioned earlier how cultural patriarchal hegemony becomes toxic when many of the men have developmental trauma disorders. Thus Cross Borders, though poorly publicised, provides a vital function in our Watikanyilpai "nurturing the nurturers" initiative. We shall be offering it all our support

Organisational Education and Policy Development

The following programs are also very important but focus more on education and policy development than service delivery.

The Australian Childhood Foundation.

Of all the Australian organisations that are trying to address childhood abuse and neglect, the Melbourne-based Australian Childhood Foundation (ACF) stands out across every domain. Its website, http://www.childhood.org.au/, is essential viewing for anyone working in these areas. The foundation was formed in 1986 with a primary aim of preventing child abuse and reducing the harm it causes by working with families and the community, providing specialist trauma counselling and therapeutic care to child victims of abuse, and running research, education, and community-awareness programs (http://www. childhood.org.au/about-us/mission-and-vision).

While ACF has a very broad scope, in 2006, it formally partnered a large group of domestic violence organisations in Victoria, including the Indigenous Family Violence Regional Action Group. The aim of this multi-agency cross-sector partnership was to develop structures and processes that effectively strengthened the coordination of responses offered by the family violence service system with respect to indigenous communities

Since 2014, it has organised biannual international conferences featuring some of the leading exponents in the field of developmental neuropsychology (practitioners and researchers like Allan Schore, Pat Ogden, Dan Siegel, Stephen Porges, Sue Carter, Ed Tronick, Martin Teicher). It offers ongoing support and training to practitioners and organisations working in the area of child trauma.

At its 2015 International Conference, it featured what we consider to be one of the most exemplary indigenous pre- and perinatal programs in Australia, the Mallee District Bumps to Babes and Beyond, which we described earlier.

Australian Childhood Foundation wants to:

- apply the evidence from neuroscience to help children heal from the hurt of abuse and neglect;
- promote and build stable and secure relationships for all children;
- work in partnership to have a collective impact on the lives of traumatised children and families;
- be relentless in advocating for the needs of children; and
- educate and empower communities to safeguard children.

The First 1000 Days Program

The Victorian Indigenous Health Equity Unit and Koori Group, Onemda, in association with Melbourne University, developed this programme in 2014, designed to enhance nutritional, social, environmental, educational, and family supports available for the developing infant and child in indigenous communities (Arabena 2014). More recently still, Jenny Munro, a nationally renowned indigenous worker based in Redfern, Sydney, has adopted the First 1000 Days programme in order to promote pre-, peri-, and postnatal nurturance for the Redfern Aboriginal community.

Commonwealth Government Community Sector Initiatives

The Australian Government Department of Health and Ageing, in its Indigenous Health Program initiatives, has established the New Directions Mothers and Babies Services (NDMBS), with which Aboriginal and Torres Strait Islander families with young children are provided access to antenatal care, standard information about baby care, practical advice, and assistance with breastfeeding nutrition and parenting. It monitors developmental milestones, immunisation status, and infections; and it undertakes health checks for Aboriginal and Torres Strait Islander children before they start school. Funding of $54 million was provided in the 2014–15 Budget to increase the number of sites providing NDMBS services from 85 to 136 (51 additional sites) over the three years to 2018. Details can be found in its online publication, *Descriptive Analysis of New Directions Mothers and Babies Services Program Final Report* (2013). The program had the input of paediatrics professor David Olds, University of Colorado, director of the Prevention Research Centre for Family and Child Health, which investigates methods of preventing health and developmental problems in children and parents from low-income families, and incorporates a more detailed understanding of advances in developmental neuroscience and attachment theory to refine its primary prevention task of nurturing the nurturers.

The Aboriginal and Torres Straits Islanders Healing Foundation

Established on the first anniversary of the Apology to Australia's Aboriginal and Torres Strait Islander peoples, the Aboriginal and Torres Strait Islander Healing Foundation is a national independent organisation with a focus on 'healing the profound legacy of pain and hurt of our people caused by colonisation, forced removals and other past government policies'. Their excellent e-publication *Growing Our Children Up Strong and Deadly: Healing for Children and Young People* (ATSI Healing Foundation 2013) is very comprehensive, and examines the latest approaches to healing intergenerational trauma experienced by Aboriginal and Torres Strait Islander children and young people. It incorporates a current understanding of neurodevelopmental advances in the understanding of the effects of trauma on the developing brain, and healing programs designed to repair this.

MOS Plus and RTS

Following the publication of *Little Children Are Sacred* (Mekarle 1992) an overview of concerns about Aboriginal Children in the Northern Territory, the Board of Inquiry into the Protection of Aboriginal Children from Sexual Abuse was established in 2006 and a service initiative, MOS Plus (Mobile Outreach Service), began visiting remote communities with a specific brief to provide help for children who were suspected of having been subjected to sexual abuse. It broadened its brief to support for Aboriginal children and their families and communities experiencing trauma associated with any form of child abuse or neglect. It continued to provide an outreach service delivering culturally safe counselling and access to external professional development and community education to increase community members' and local agencies' understanding of child abuse and related trauma. More recently, it combined with Community Child Safety and Wellbeing Teams and the Remote Aboriginal Family and Community Program as an overarching service now called RTS (Remote Therapeutic Family Support Service). In our work in remote communities, we established a close linkage with their personnel and their programs. We were very pleased that they had been accessing the Australian Childhood Foundation facilities and training programs and bringing an understanding of recent advances in developmental neuroscience and a therapeutic approach based on a deep understanding of empathy and mindfulness practices, but we learned on a recent visit to the region that funding had been withdrawn, again illustrating how the political process devalues early nurturance!

Nurturing the Nurturers in Indigenous Communities: Preliminary Reflections and Recommendations

Even though little can be found in the major religions by way of a focused understanding of the first two or so years of life, the principle of pre-, peri-, and postnatal nurturance is an ancient one found across many cultures. The term *doula* (derived from the Ancient Greek for 'female helper or servant') was first used by the anthropologist Dana Raphael but has since come to be used for a worldwide range of organisations offering perinatal nurturance support. There is a good discussion of doula issues and effects in Koumouitzes-Douvia et al. (2006).

As we have said earlier, there are obviously some very sensitive issues in effective delivery. Many of the young women, because of their own developmental histories, will inevitably have difficult attachment dynamics (like avoidant, anxious, or disorganised patterns), which make it very difficult to deliver acceptable nurturance unless the support workers themselves have well developed mindfulness and empathy function, an understanding of attachment dynamics and patterns, and a good deal of cultural awareness, including indigenous nurturance (*kanyini*) traditions.

The nurturers (usually mothers who have come through immense difficulties in their own infancies and often continue to live in extremely stressful environments) are both sensitive and sensitised. Caring professionals need to bring a range of mindfulness- and empathy-based skills to this delicate but crucial task. And these awarenesses need to be developed across the social spectrum—the health and child care / protection service, management in the organisations that sustain these services, and the political processes that ultimately fund them. Recently in Central Australia, funding continuity for a Primary Preventative Mental Health Program to remote communities was threatened. What was at stake was the therapeutic alliances that had been established with patients over years by personnel with high levels of social/emotional intelligence and cultural awareness. Disrupting these therapeutic alliances would inevitably result in a resurgence of suicides and psychiatric relapses. But the fund providers seemed either to have no grasp of this, or naively imagined that a Lego system of interchangeable personnel would save the day.

Some Recommendations

Some of our earlier case vignettes made reference to a range of useful intervention. Here is an attempt to organize these in a more coherent fashion.

Our recommendation for mental health personnel working with indigenous mothers and children include:

- indigenous cultural and language training, 'Dreaming' stories;
- training in mindfulness and empathy-based therapeutic processes, including the building of therapeutic alliances;
- training in preverbal/nonverbal communications;
- awareness of their own attachment styles;
- organizational support for sustaining 'long enough' therapeutic alliances;

- accessing the Babes to Bumps and Beyond Program for modelling and mentoring (Burrows et al. 2014).

Additional Programmes of Repair

Had we been better resourced, there are two further measures we would have introduced in our work with BC.

1. Singing and music. There is a good review by the music therapist Marianne Bargiel (2004) on the positive impact of singing and attachment in infants.

2. Neurofeedback. Sebern Fisher (2014), who is in close communication with the senior author, is one of the world's leading authorities on the use of specific neurofeedback protocols aimed at reducing amygdalar overactivity in developmental trauma disorders, thereby accessing neuroplastic therapeutic possibilities that are not readily available with even the most skilful language-based psychotherapies. Some neurofeedback work with our patient could have made our supportive interventions even more effective.

3. Sensory Motor Psychotherapy. Developmental trauma disorder, because it has its origins in the first three years of life, has a strong preverbal component and presents with many physical sensations which precipitate intense trauma-related emotions of terror and helplessness. It needs a form of psychotherapy which can address this that works directly with the client's embodied experience.
   Pat Ogden is a psychotherapist and researcher who founded the Sensorimotor Psychotherapy Institute in Boulder, Colorado. The Australian Childhood Foundation, in conjunction with Pat Ogden's

Sensorimotor Psychotherapy Institute, offers training in this method, to engage traumatised mothers and their children more effectively (Ogden and Fisher 2015).

Health organizations need to incorporate these awarenesses so that the empathic engagement processes can resonate across the support system (in our case, local clinic staff, indigenous workers, obstetrics and pre- and postnatal staff, mental health staff, tertiary consultation facilities like SwOPS). Most importantly, workers and services can encourage and support indigenous initiatives to establish such services.

Wrapping It Up

Disadvantaged indigenous communities have been suffering from a transgenerational cascade of developmental trauma with all its awful physical and mental consequences, virtually since first contact with Western invasion. Much of this contact has been highly traumatic (genocides, dispossessions, destruction of culture, the impact of alcohol and drugs, etc.),

But even when Western approaches have been more benign, they have been characterised by mindlessness, an inability to accurately empathise with their objects. There is a huge amount of repair to be done.

On the positive side, however, we now know, much more confidently thanks to our advanced developmental neuropsychological understanding, what is likely to work. This chapter has described some positive examples and what stands out are some recent initiatives from the indigenous sector itself, like the Babes to Bumps and Beyond programme. Not only are they starting to heal the damage and prevent further damage, but they are of such high quality that they can serves as inspirations and role models for the broader community.

> *Finally, Wati Kanyilpai asks us to join with him to extend our deepest gratitude to the elders of the Papunya, Inkuntji, Watiyawanu and Walungurru communities in Central Australia for their ongoing mentoring and encouragement.*

BIBLIOGRAPHY

1. Allen, B., Watson, M. 'Bumps to Babes and Beyond: Improving Outcomes for Young Aboriginal Women and Their Children'. Presentation at the 2014 Child Trauma International Conference, Melbourne, August 6, 2014, and ARACY at http://www.iecsewc2013.net.au/presentations/BBB-presentation-ARACY-2013.pdf.

2. Arabena, K. (2014). The 'First 1,000 Days': Implementing Strategies across Victorian Government Agencies to Improve the Health and Wellbeing Outcomes for Aboriginal Children and their Families, Indigenous Health Equity Unit, The University of Melbourne, Melbourne. http://www.onemda.unimelb.edu.au/first1000days.

3. Arney, F., Bowering, K., Chong, A., Healy, V., Volkmer, B. (2010). 'Sustained Nurse Home Visiting with Families of Aboriginal Children'. In Arney, F., and Scott, D., eds., *Working with Vulnerable Families: A Partnership Approach.* Port Melbourne, Vic.: Cambridge University Press. 9780521744461: 109-134,

4. Australian Institute of Health and Welfare (2015). 'Closing the Gap: Foetal Alcohol Spectrum Disorders; A Review of Interventions for Prevention and Management in Indigenous Communities'. *Resource sheet no. 36* prepared by the Closing the Gap Clearinghouse. ISSN 2201-845X, ISBN 978-1-74249-685-6. Cat. no. IHW 148.

5. Bargiel, M. (2004). *Lullabies and Play Songs. Theoretical Considerations for an Early Attachment Music Therapy Intervention*

through Parental Singing for Developmentally At-Risk Infants. Voices: A World Forum for Music Therapy. https://normt. uib.no/index.php/voices/article/viewArticle/149/125.

6. Burrows, A., Allen, B., Gorton, S. (2014). *Bumps to Babes and Beyond Evaluation Program.* Pdf accessible at **http:// tinyurl.com/ndawafq.**

7. Cargo, M., and Warner, L. (2013). '"Realist Evaluation" in Action: A Worked Example of the Aboriginal Parental Engagement Program'. *CFCA Connect.* Murdoch Children's Research Institute, Aboriginal Health Council of South Australia. Melbourne, Vic.: Murdoch Children's Research Institute.

8. Cozolino, L. (2006). *The Neuroscience of Human Relationships: Attachment and the Developing Social Brain.* 269–73. W. W. Norton & Co., New York,

9. De Bellis, M., and Thomas, L. (2003). 'Biologic Findings of Post-Traumatic Stress Disorder and Child Maltreatment'. *Current Psychiatry Reports*, 5, 108–117.

10. De Bellis, M., Keshavan, M., Clark, D., Casey, B., Giedd, J., Boring, A., Frustaci, K., and Ryan, N. (1999). 'Developmental Traumatology, Part II: Brain Development'. *Biological Psychiatry*, 45, 1271–1284.

11. Elliott-Farrelly, T. (2004). 'Australian Aboriginal Suicide: The Need for an Aboriginal Suicidology?' *Advances in Mental Health, Vol. 3: Indigenous Mental Health*, pp. 138–145. doi: 10.5172/jamh.3.3.138.

12. Fisher, S. (2014). *Neurofeedback in the Treatment of Developmental Trauma: Calming the Fear-Driven Brain*. Norton. NY.

13. Fonagy, P. (2004). 'Psychotherapy Meets Neuroscience: A More Focused Future for Psychotherapy Research'. *Psychiatric Bulletin*, 2 8, 357–359.

14. Harris, K. R., and Bucens, I. K. (2003). 'Prevalence of Foetal Alcohol Syndrome in the Top End of the Northern Territory'. *Journal of Paediatrics and Child Health* 39:528–533.

15. John, A. P., Koloth, R., Dragovic, M., Lim, S. C. B. (2009). 'Prevalence of Metabolic Syndrome among Australians with Severe Mental Illness'. *Med J. Aust.* 190 (4): 176–179.

16. Koumouitzes-Douvia, J., CARR, C. A. (2006). 'Women's Perceptions of Their Doula Support'. *J. Perinat. Educ.* Fall; 15(4): 34–40. doi: 10.1624/105812406X151402. PMCID: PMC1804309.

17. Lee, L., Griffiths, C., Glossop, P., and Eapen, V. (2010). 'The Boomerangs Parenting Program for Aboriginal Parents and Their Young Children'. *Australasian Psychiatry* v. 18 no. 6: 527–533.

18. Manne, A. (2005) *Motherhood: How Should We Care for Our Children?* Allen & Unwin.

19. Manne, A., personal communication, 2012.

20. Marmot, M. (2005). 'Social Determinants of Health Inequalities'. *The Lancet*, Volume 365, Issue 9464, Pages 1099–1104.

21. McGowan, P. O., Sasaki, A., D'Alession, A. C., Dymov, S., Labonté, B., Szyf, M., Turecki, G., Meaney, M. J. (2009). 'Epigenetic Regulation of the Glucocorticoid Receptor in Human Brain Associates with Childhood Abuse'. *Nat. Neurosci.* 12 (3):342–8. March. doi:10.1038/nn.2270. PMC 2944040. PMID 19234457.

22. Meaney, M. J. (2001). 'Maternal Care, Gene Expression, and the Transmission of Individual Differences in Stress Reactivity across Generations'. *Annu. Rev. Neurosci.* **24**: 1161–92. doi:10.1146/annurev.neuro.24.1.1161. PMID 11520931.

23. Narvaez, D., Panksepp, J., Schore, A., Gleason, T., eds. (2013). *Evolution, Early Experience and Human Development: From Research to Practice and Policy.* Oxford University Press 2013.

24. Pearson, N. (2010). 'Nights When I Dream of a Better World: Moving from the Centre-Left to the Radical Centre of Australian Politics'. Swinburne Institute for Social Research website. Posted 7 September 2010. Retrieved 4 February 2013.

25. Petchkovsky, L, Scholem, L. S, Ashley, J. J., Kirkby, R. J. (1975) 'An Attempt to Transfer Drug-induced Activity via Brain Matter', in *Journal of Biological Psychology.* MHRI Ann Arbor, Michigan. Sept.

26. Petchkovsky, L.; San Roque, C. (2002). 'Tjunguwyiangka; Attacks on Linking; Forced Separation and Its Psychiatric Sequelae in Australia's Stolen Generation'. *Journal of Transcultural Psychiatry*, Vol. 39, No. 3, Pp. 345–366, September.

27. Petchkovsky, L., Cord-Udy, N., Grant, L. (2007). 'A Post-Jungian Perspective on 55 Indigenous Suicides in Central Australia; Deadly Cycles of Diminished Resilience, Impaired Nurturance, Compromised Interiority; and Possibilities for Repair. *Australian e-Journal for the Advancement of Mental Health* (*AeJAMH*), Volume 6, Issue 3, 2007. ISSN: 1446-7984.

28. Petchkovsky, L., San Roque, C., Jurra Napaljari, R., Butler, S. (2004). 'Indigenous Maps of Subjectivity and Attacks on Linkage: Forced Separation and Its Psychiatric Sequelae in Australia's Stolen Generations'. *AeJAMH*, Vol 3, Issue 3. ISSN 1446-7984.

29. Petchkovsky, L. (1982). 'Images of Madness in Australian Aborigines'. *Journal of Analytical Psychology*, 27, 21–39, 1982.

30. 'Politics of Nurturance'. https://watikanyilpai.wordpress.com/.

31. Porges, S.W. (2011). *The Polyvagal Theory: Neurophysiological Foundations of Emotions, Attachment, Communication, Self-Regulation.* Norton. NY.

32. Price, J. (2018). 'Ngajurlangu: Me Too' (essay). *Meanjin*. Vol 77, 4. December.

33. Rickwood, D., White, A., Eckersley, R. (2007). 'Overview of Current Trends in Mental Health Problems for Australia's Youth and Adolescents'. *Clinical Psychologist.* Volume 11, Issue 3, 2007. Special Issue: Youth Mental Health. Pages 72–78

34. Rothwell, N. (2014). 'Lesson of the Direct Approach'. In the *Weekend Australian* June 21–22, pp. 13 and 18.

35. Rothwell, N. (2013), in the *Weekend Australian* (June 1–2).

36. Schore, A. N. (2003). *Affect Regulation and the Repair of the Self.* Norton N.Y.

37. Siegel, D. (2007). *The Mindful Brain*, see especially pp. 159–62. Norton NY.

38. Siegel, D. (2011). *Mindsight: The New Science of Personal Transformation.* Bantam Books. New York. Passim.

39. Taylor, R. (2003). 'Whitewash: On Keith Windschuttle's Fabrication of Aboriginal History', in *On Keith Windschuttle's Fabrication of Aboriginal History.* Edited by Robert Manne. Black Inc. Agenda, October 25.

40. Trudgen, R. (2000). *When Warriors Lie Down and Die.* Aboriginal Resources and Development Services Inc. Parap. NT.

41. Van der Kolk, B. A., Pynoos, R. S., Cicchetti, D., Cloitre, M., D'Andrea, W., Ford, J. D., Lieberman, A. F., Putnam, F. W., Saxe, G., Spinazzola, J., Stolbach, B. C., Teicher, M. (2009). *Proposal to include a developmental trauma disorder diagnosis for children and adolescents in DSM-5.* http://www.traumacenter.org/announcements/DTD_papers_Oct_09.pdf.

42. Van der Kolk, B. A. (2014) The Body Keeps the Score: *Brain, Mind, and Body in the Healing of Trauma.* Viking Books.

43. Walker, J., McDonald, D. (1995) *The Over-Representation of Indigenous People in Custody in Australia.* August. Australian

Institute of Criminology, GPO Box 2944, Canberra ACT 260, Australia.ISSN 0817-8542.ISBN 0 642 23323 3.

44. Wirraka Maya (2015). Health Service Dreamtime Project. August. http://www.abc.net.au/news/2015-08-05/new-program-to-help-aboriginal-mothers-bond-with-their-babies/6675088.

45. Yeo Soo See (2003). Child Abuse Review, Volume 12, Issue 5, pages 292–304, September/October.

46. Lofthouse, L., Arnold, E., Hersch, S., Hurt, E., deBeus, R. (2011). 'A Review of Neurofeedback Treatment for Pediatric ADHD'. *Journal of Attention Disorders*. Vol. 16, Issue 5, pp. 351–372. https://doi.org/10.1177/1087054711427530.

47. Dadds, M. R., Allen, J. L., Oliver, B. R., Faulkner, N., Legge, K., Moul, C., Woolgar, M., Scott, S. (2012). 'Love, Eye Contact and the Developmental Origins of Empathy v. Psychopathy'. *The British Journal of Psychiatry* Mar, 200 (3) 191–196; DOI: 10.1192/bjp.bp.110.085720.

48. Steiner, N. J., Frenette, E. C., Rene, K. M., Brennan, R. T. (2104). In-School Neurofeedback Training for ADHD: Sustained Improvements from a Randomized Control Trial. *Am. Acad. Pediatrics. Pediatrics* Volume 133, Number 3, March 2014.).

- We thank Professor Philip Boyce and his SWOP Team for their sensitive support.
- BC has given us a signed approval for placing the photo in a publication.

CHAPTER 5

Fixing It Up

Climate change is threatening the global ecosystem. The consequences to the next few generations will be dire unless we can improve things. There are, of course, some climate change deniers, but at least, they recognise there is something to deny.

Not so with global nurturance malfunctions. As we have described in detail, developmental trauma disorders have disastrous consequences for the individual; all those physical, emotional, behavioural, psychological and cognitive problems we have described in detail in Chapter 3. And these problems, in turn, make impacts on the wider society. The global sociocultural sphere needs repair.

But the problem is so *off* the global radar that there are not even any nurturance deniers!

It is time to come with Wati Kanyilpai on the final leg of our journey: *How do we fix it all up?*

We will be looking **especially from the male perspective** at (1) what we can do to repair our own developmental traumas and become better nurturers (2) how we can then extend this to the wider world the family, the various helping organisations, and the political system.

The contents of this chapter need a separate book; there is just so much material. But we need to make a start somewhere.

We are all so overburdened, as if there isn't already so much on our backs. But working on developing nurturance is good for you individually, as well as for the planet. Persevere; it pays big dividends. Despite all the difficulties, there are many people on this planet who had a background of developmental trauma but made constructive lives for themselves in various helping and healing professions.

We all come into the world through our mothers, whether we are boys or girls. One vital task for men is to integrate their feminine aspect. Carl Jung was onto this, with his concept of the anima, the feminine in every man, recommending that men take particular notice of the female figures that appear in men's dreams. My Canadian colleague Ozaway Pinesse (do google him) puts it well in this picture.

All indigenous
cultures
understand
the role of
woman as
trancendant
mediator.

She brings us all
into the world,
she is the link
between past
and present.

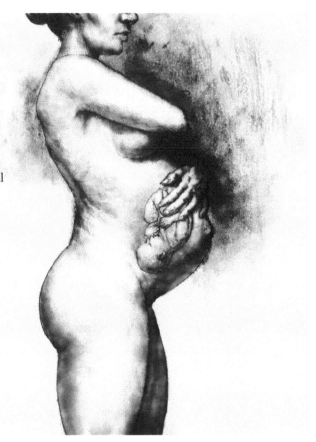

Men—Fixing *Ourselves* Up: What We Can Do to Repair Our Own Developmental Traumas and Become Better Nurturers

Let us start with *ourselves*. I often tell my patients that the most selfish thing anyone can do is to extend loving-kindness to someone else. How can this be? When we extend love to other beings, we have to use what Dan Siegel calls the 'resonance circuits', brain networks that involve our mirror neurones, which extend that love to ourselves as we are sending to out to others. .

It also works the other way around. When we extend loving-kindness to ourselves, this makes it easier for the brain to extend that to others.

As we have said so many times before, to be good carers, the two BIG factors we need to develop are (1) *mindfulness* and (2) *empathy*. We will also look at (3) a wide range of closely connected procedures and practices, including psychotherapy, that will help us feel better and be more competent carers.

Developing Mindfulness

Mindfulness Practices

Mindfulness practices are many and varied, but again can be boiled down to two basic procedures. The first is (1) concentration practice. One brings one's focus to a particular object, a mantra, a visual object, or a sensation (like the natural breath). As one's attention and concentration become stronger, awareness of the elements of the experience become subtler and more refined. Concentration practice develops the internal 'microscope', which can then be brought to awareness of the 'now', the present moment, microsecond to microsecond. This of course is the (2) second strand of mindfulness practice.

Concentration Practice

The initial stages of training emphasize the development of powerful concentration. The student begins by focusing on the breath (usually the sensations in the lower abdomen as it moves in respiration). At first, one can count the breaths and then later simply watch it. With intensive practice, concentration becomes so strong that a state of 'one-pointedness' (the so-called *jhana*) is achieved.

Even though I've been doing intensive meditation practices for over forty years, I'm still a very poor meditator, but if I am doing a month long intensive retreat, I can occasionally get to a point where awareness of the breath occupies the entire awareness field, becomes completely effortless, and is accompanied by feelings of intense serenity . . . albeit for a few minutes only.

Once concentration practice has become powerful, the 'microscope' of mindful awareness can be usefully brought to bear on other phenomena.

One of them is focusing on the now, the present moment, aware of what passes through the mind and in one's surroundings in the present moment. The Zen term for this is *Shikantaza*.

Mindfulness in essence is awareness of what is going on in self and environment, but it operates at many levels, some of them very subtle. Many of us tend to function in robotic mode, driven by whatever brain program is active at the time.

And without mindfulness, genuine empathy is impossible.

We work with this all the time in psychotherapy. My patient Jill, a victim of sexual abuse by her father, says to me:

> *I hate your wife. I think she tells you all the time that I am trying to seduce you . . . and I hate you, because you listen to her.*

I spend some time acknowledging how bad she feels, the hurt, the anger, the shame . . . and then I say:

> *I wonder how your mother felt about your father's abuse?*

There's a long silence, and then:

> *She said it was **my** fault, I was too flirtatious.*

She smiles . . . Jill has moved from being driven mindlessly by a traumatic program to bringing mindful awareness to her process. She's made the connection between her history of abuse and her feelings about my wife.

Cultivating Empathy

What is this thing we call empathy? It is the capacity to tune in to others in a clear and loving way. There are two aspects to empathy. One of them is what we call *perspectival* empathy. The other is *emotional* empathy. Psychopaths are very good at perspectival empathy. They read you like a menu, all the better to eat you. But there's no love. The psychopath psychiatrist, Hannibal Lecter, in *Silence of the Lambs*, does exactly that: he reads you, all the better to eat you.

People with autism, on the other hand, struggle with perspectival empathy, the ability to tune into what is going on in other beings. But when they DO tune in, they do so in an emotional way.

What is required is an intellectual awareness of the internal processes of others, coupled with kindness.

What Do Meditation Practices Teach Us about These Two Factors?

Mindfulness practices and loving-kindness/empathy practices are intimately connected. Deep mindfulness practices rest on a base of radical openness. Radical openness is another way of describing deep love. And in turn, unadulterated love can only exist in a state of absolute awareness. It has often been remarked by a range of meditation teachers that loving-kindness has 'near enemies', which look like it but are actually subtly different. Erotic and romantic feelings can feel very strong, as do a range of other kinds of attachment. At first attachment may feel just like love. But as it grows, it becomes more clearly the opposite, characterised by clinging and controlling and fear. The same is true of compassion, whose 'near enemy' is pity, which feels sorry for that poor person over there as if he were somehow different from us.

Thus mindful awareness/concentration practices need to be complemented with loving-kindness practices, because without loving-kindness, equanimity becomes indifference and detachment. Compassion gets lost. People can develop strong concentration practices while failing to develop loving-kindness and this merely allows them to be more efficient killers, like Pol Pot, the Cambodian despot who had studied as a Buddhist monk.

The usual Pali term for loving-kindness is **metta**.

Loving-Kindness Practice

Here is a simple *metta* meditation.

1. Find a comfortable position sit in.
2. Bring your awareness to the midline of the body, the heart and chest.
3. Bring to mind some STRONG kindly act or love that you have received in life from a friend, a parent, and animal, whatever.
4. See how that feels in your heart region. Expand it.
5. Then send it to yourself. You may add the following words or something similar: *May I be well, may I be happy, may I be peaceful, may I be full of love and compassion.*

There is a huge range of meditation/loving-kindness resources (of varying qualities) to be found on the net. Try some of them, and if you find something that hits the spot, practice at least twenty minutes of it every day.

I strongly recommend Dr Daniel Siegel's Wheel of Awareness practice. This covers the field in a way that is easily accessible to a Westerner.

Go to http://www.drdansiegel.com/resources/wheel_of_awareness/ and download his three free audio guided meditations. Dan has also written a new book on the subject called *Aware: The Science and Practice of Presence* (Siegel 2018).

Try a Meditation Retreat

Start off with a day or a weekend. If you have had a difficult childhood and score high on the ACE test (see further on in this chapter for the questionnaire), you will need to be careful with this. Just do a few days at first. A long meditation retreat for somehow who has developmental trauma can sometimes bring on a psychotic episode. One needs to develop a strong ego before one can lose it.

And Now for the Children

Now that you know how to meditate, you can teach the children. The Dalai Lama is on record as saying that if we could only teach our all children how to meditate when they turned eight, the next generation would be one of world peace, love, and harmony. So teach them to meditate, please, as well as doing whatever you can to help them have a good first three years of life.

Some Other Things You Can Do to Enhance Empathy

Do Twenty-Second Hugs

These raise oxytocin (the bonding hormone) and lower cortisol, norepinephrine, and blood pressure stressor responses (Grewen, Girdler, Amico, and Light 2005). The more of this you do, the better you get at empathy and extending loving-kindness.

The Importance of Touch

Recent work by the neuroscientist David Linden at John Hopkins School of Medicine reminds us that brain networks have evolved in human that activate specifically in response to the experience of a caress (2015). Infants deprived of touch, like the Romanian orphans, are left with severe dysfunctions.

Touch is sociopolitically problematic across a range of domains. In a bid to reduce paedophilia, legislation has been passed in many countries prohibiting teachers from touching their pupils in the school environment. And in most forms of psychotherapy, especially psychoanalysis, touch has long been regarded as a 'boundary violation'. There is also a range of proscriptions against touch in various circumstances in various religions. For instance, the Vinaya Pitaka, the texts that prescribe behaviour for Buddhist monks, includes prohibitions against touching women. We can understand the concerns that might underlie these prohibitions. In psychoanalysis, we can get around these to some extent by *talking* about touch and, maybe at an appropriate moment, even making comments like 'I'm giving you a big mental hug' without following through with an actual physical enactment that would constitute a boundary violation.

Yet haptics, the term for any form of interaction involving touch, is central to the neurodevelopmental processes of attachment in the infant. Kindly touch is vital in the preverbal stage of development. Its value needs to be sensitively considered and deployed in any 'nurturing the nurturers' programme.

Rocking

Contemporary research has looked at the way babies need lots of rocking. It helps develop the relational networks in the brain. Try this whenever you hug someone. Dancing is also a good way of incorporating this into our daily lives.

Music

Music works largely on right-hemisphere circuits. It is especially effective when done in groups. The rhythm and the prosody turn down right amygdalar hyperactivity, and the resonance that gets established between the members of the group activates relational circuits.

My music therapist colleague Kirstin Robertson-Gillam and I ran a twelve-week choir group with some chronically depressed people who were all hypervigilant and various ways. We did QEEGs before and after, and found that their P3a wave (an indicator of brain hypervigilance) normalised over those twelve weeks (Robertson-Gillam and Petchovsky 2012)

Do eye contact.

See Christian Jarrett on *Research Digest* (2016) and Victoria Leong (2017), who have both done a lot of work in this field.

When a parent and infant interact, various aspects of their behaviour can synchronise, including their gaze, emotions, and heart rate, but now we also know that the electrical brain activity of both of them tends to synchronise, and this makes for better empathy.

Eye contact can be challenging, but studies show that brain synchronisation during eye contact is also true for adults. Thus when adults are talking to each other, communication is more successful if their brainwaves are in synchrony, which happens with eye contact.

Develop Some Reflective Listening Skills

This is so important. It allows you to develop empathic connections with adults and children, using both sides of the brain—the verbal left hemisphere and the emotional/relational right hemisphere. And as you get better at it, both you and the person you are interacting with feel better. But it takes a lot of practice.

Carl Rogers, fifty years ago, knew that tuning in to the person through reflective listening was much more useful than all the interpretation / advice-giving / clever responses. It gives the other person a sense of being caringly reflected, so that they can process their own internal states more fully.

Let me give you an example.

You are with your six-year-old daughter. She has been playing with a doll, and you notice she is upset. Try to read her body language. Her lips and her eyes are tight; she has a frown on her face. Her body is shaking a bit (right-brain stuff). You put it into words (left brain) and say

You're feeling upset.

She replies,

My dolly's leg is broken.

You then repeat what she says, and expand on it to cover feelings.

Your dolly's leg is broken, and you feel hurt.

She corrects you.

No, I'm angry!

You reflect that back to her.

You're angry.

Note what is happening. Because you are reflecting her states back to her (1), this allows her to better tune into what is going for her, to identify her processes more accurately. You are helping her develop better quality mindfulness. Because you are in tune with her (2), she feels more secure and safe to express herself more fully. And she goes on;

> *Jack [her younger brother] was playing with it and broke it.*

You reflect back

You're angry with Jack.

She replies,

Yes, he's always breaking my toys.

You can repeat that back to her and add some feelings.

He's always breaking your toys, and you feel hurt.

She says,

Yes, I feel so sad.

Note that you have healed her connect with sad feelings, which she was avoiding earlier because she was overwhelmed with anger. You have helped her increase her mindfulness even further.

As you continue with more reflective listening, she gets a chance to unload painful feelings, and begin to feel better. This then allows her to develop some solutions.

Why don't you get me a toy box that I can lock up, so that he can't get at them?

She's figured out that Jack can't control himself much, an empathic reflection. The end result is much better than a temper tantrum; it has more mindfulness, more empathy, more resourcefulness.

Here is another example.

My granddaughter Irene (aged five) is driving a little pedal car. Her brother Owen (aged three) wants to drive the car and is harassing her, throwing a huge temper tantrum. I say to him,

You are very angry with Irene. You really want to drive the car so much.

Irene says,

He could ask more nicely.

Owen responds,

NURTURING THE NURTURERS; HEALING THE PLANET

*Dear Irene, can I **please** drive the car?*

Irene gets out of the car and hands the controls over to him. She then goes to the bedroom and has a cry. I follow her and say,

You are so upset, but you are such a kind girl.

She cries some more as I empathise/reflectively listen further, and finally, she settles and says,

Yes, I was kind to him. I'm a good girl.

Owen comes into her room and tells her she can have the car back.

Reflective Listening with Your Partner

Good reflective listening takes time and effort to develop. One **big** difficulty is if both you and your partner are very upset at the same time. Neither of you can bring reflective listening to each other.

It may be possible for you to put your own hurt on the back burner to deal with later, and you can then do some reflective listening with her.

> *You are angry with me because I left the pizza in the oven and it is burnt.*

She replies,

> *But you do things like that all the time, you just don't think about my needs.*

You reflect back,

You feel unloved, uncared for by me.

She replies,

*Well, no, I think you **do** care about me, but the pizza burning brought back memories of how often my mother used to neglect me, as if I wasn't there or didn't matter.*

And she starts to cry. At which point, you can take things further and encourage her to have a good cry and be kind to herself while she is doing that. She will usually feel relieved, and you both will have avoided yet another futile argument.

When we cry, the tears actually carry a lot of ACTH (adrenocorticotrophic hormone) away from the brain. Getting rid of this major stress hormone makes us feel better. Many women intuitively know this and will put on a sad DVD in the afternoon so they can have a good cry, because they know that will feel so much better afterwards. Sometimes you are just too upset to be able to do reflective listening. Crying can help soothing yourself.

Do be aware that if you are always expecting the *other* person to do all the emotional caring, you are locking yourself into what we psychotherapists call the 'victim' pattern.

Victim, Persecutor, and Rescuer: The So-Called Drama Triangle

Many people on this planet seem to be locked into this very unhelpful pattern. It gives them an illusion of autonomy and control but, in fact, keeps them lodged in negative states. And it makes for inoperable relationships. It emerges with incidents of developmental trauma encountered during the counterdependent stage of development.

A two-year-old will go through a stage of saying no or refusing to obey as part of the normal process of establishing independence and separateness from his mother/attachment figure. When the mother has difficulty accepting the child's need for active distancing, the child may remain stuck in this counterdependent phase of development. Most of their relationship patterns will then be drama triangle ones: playing the victim, being the persecutor, or trying to deal with this by playing rescuer.

The drama triangle pattern is well described in a book by my colleagues Janae and Barry Weinhold (2013) in their book *Breaking Free of the Drama Triangle and Victim Consciousness*, which look at how to deal with this matter and how to best resolve it.

Here is a brief description of the three role states in this harmful triangle.

1. **The victim.** Feels oppressed, helpless, hopeless, powerless, ashamed, and seems unable to make decisions, solve problems, or achieve insight. In the victim role, the tendency is to actually seek out persecutors and also rescuers. This merely perpetuates negative feelings.

2. **The persecutor.** In this role state, one is controlling, blaming, critical, oppressive, angry, authoritative, rigid, and superior. The persecutor's mentality is "**It's** *all your fault.*"

3. **The rescuer.** One problem with this role is that, when it is habitual, it often becomes a way of avoiding dealing with one's own issues. The other problem is that it tends to have negative effects on the victims that one is trying to rescue, keeping them dependent, rather than encouraging them to develop more autonomy.

People caught up in this triangle spend much of their time moving from one role to the other. Robert and Janae offer some very effective ways of moving beyond this.

Here is what the Weinholds (2013) say about not engaging in someone's victim role as rescuer or persecutor.

> 1. Reflect back their feelings when [people in the Victim role] complain or accuse you. This lets them know that you are listening and that you care about them.
>
> 2. Then ask them, '*What do you want from me?*' This is a real 'drama-stopper!'
>
> (a). Making people ask for what they want forces them to stop whining and complaining. (b). They must think about what they want from you. Often, they don't even know.
>
> 3. If they don't know what they want from you, say, '*Well, think about what you need. When you know, ask me for what you need.*' Once they do know what they do want or need, they must ask you for it directly.

Try it out next time your partner does a 'victim' performance. Then try it again, and again. This needs lots of practice. But in the end, helps YOU, HER, and the RELATIONSHIP.

Do the Adverse Childhood Events Questionnaire

Get some sense of how much developmental trauma you may be carrying.

Wikipedia explains things well. I quote:

> The Adverse Childhood Experiences Study (ACE Study) is a research study conducted by the American health maintenance organization Kaiser Permanente and the Centers for Disease Control and Prevention. Participants were recruited to the study between 1995 and 1997 and have been in long-term follow up for health outcomes. The study has demonstrated an association of adverse childhood experiences (ACEs) with health and social problems as an adult. The study is frequently cited as a notable landmark in epidemiological research, and has produced more than 50 scientific articles and more than 100 conference and workshop presentations that look at the prevalence and consequences of high ACE Scores (See Felitti and Anda et al. 1998).

Adverse Childhood Experience (ACE) Questionnaire

While you were growing up, during your first eighteen years of life:

1. Did a parent or other adult in the household **often** . . .
Swear at you, insult you, put you down, or humiliate you?
or
Act in a way that made you afraid that you might be physically hurt?
Yes No If yes enter 1 _____
2. Did a parent or other adult in the household **often** . . .
Push, grab, slap, or throw something at you?
or
Ever hit you so hard that you had marks or were injured?
Yes No If yes enter 1 _____
3. Did an adult or person at least five years older than you **ever** . . .
Touch or fondle you or have you touch their body in a sexual way?
or
Try to or actually have oral, anal, or vaginal sex with you?
Yes No If yes enter 1 _____
4. Did you **often** feel that . . .
No one in your family loved you or thought you were important or special?
or
Your family didn't look out for each other, feel close to each other, or support each other?
Yes No If yes enter 1 _____
5. Did you **often** feel that . . .
You didn't have enough to eat, had to wear dirty clothes, and had no one to protect you?
or
Your parents were too drunk or high to take care of you or take you to the doctor if you needed it?
Yes No If yes enter 1 _____
6. Were your parents **ever** separated or divorced?

Yes No If yes enter 1 _____
7. Was your mother or stepmother:
Often pushed, grabbed, slapped, or had something thrown at her?
or
Sometimes or often kicked, bitten, hit with a fist, or hit with something hard?
or
Ever repeatedly hit over at least a few minutes or threatened with a gun or knife?
Yes No If yes enter 1 _____
8. Did you live with anyone who was a problem drinker or alcoholic or who used street drugs?
Yes No If yes enter 1 _____
9. Was a household member depressed or mentally ill or did a household member attempt suicide?
Yes No If yes enter 1 _____
10. Did a household member go to prison?
Yes No If yes enter 1 _____

Now add up your 'Yes' answers. This is your ACE Score. Getting 4 or more spells trouble.

There is also a **resilience questionnaire**. You can find it at http://resiliencyquiz.com/index.shtml.

If you score high on that, it can compensate somewhat for a high ACE.

Get Some Psychotherapy

If you score high on the adverse childhood events scale and have some degree of developmental trauma, then I strongly urge you to consider getting some psychotherapy.

It can be difficult to find a good practitioner. Try out two or three initial sessions with the psychotherapist, and if you feel that it is too much of a struggle, try someone else, until you find a practitioner that you feel you can work with comfortably. Sometimes it's a matter of personal idiosyncrasy. Even if your practitioner was Carl Jung himself, if you and he were somehow neurologically incompatible, things may not work out. This sometimes happens with mothers whose babies are neurologically programmed in ways that clash with the mother so that, no matter how good the mother is, developing relational intimacy—what professor of psychiatry Russell Meares calls the protoconversation between mother and infant, is a struggle. He describes this in detail in his book *Borderline Personality Disorder and the Conversational Model: A Clinician's Manual* (2012).

Be aware that even very effective psychotherapy for developmental trauma can take years. Also be aware that things *can* be accelerated with specific neurofeedback protocols of the kind recommended by Sebern Fisher, one of the world's foremost practitioners in this field. Look her up on www. sebernfisher.com/, and read her book on the subject (2014).

A Big Problem with Books

The skills that need to be imparted (mindfulness, empathy) are right-brain functions, hence nonverbal. This book, a left-brained product, cannot do it by itself. What is required is right-brain training; miming, prosody, and body language. How to do this?

We have mentioned a few ways above whereby this preverbal, subverbal domain can be fostered.

Hang out with babies and infants. Babies are your best teachers. They are nonverbal, so you have to relate to them with your right brain: gestures, prosody, attunement, empathy, loving-kindness.

And involvement in a music group (dance group, band, choir, whatever) is another fast, safe way of getting some healing.

Moving to the Wider World, Families, Social Groups, Organisations, Religion, Politics

The Bigger Picture, from Men's Perspective

Extending our focus now to the larger environment, we acknowledge that life on this planet is inherently difficult. Even if all the children on earth had good enough nurturance in the first three years of their lives, life would still bring us awful challenges, and some of the children would still grow up to be dysfunctional adults. But on the positive side, many more of them would turn out to be empathic and nurturing beings.

The notion of 'critical mass' applies here. If there are enough beings on this planet with empathy and mindfulness skills (the critical mass), we might just begin to come to terms with violence, wars, climate damage, grotesque poverty. I have no idea what the critical mass needs to be, nor does anyone else as far as I can see. Is it 25 percent of the earth's population? Fifty percent? Who knows? What is clear though is that currently, we have not arrived at critical mass: global warming, social inequity, wars and terrorism, all these still plague us. We need to nurture the nurturers to ensure a critical mass.

It is obvious that a project to nurture the nurturers needs the men on this planet to take a major part. Men are part of the problem, and men are part of the solution. As a male, I am well aware of that.

Thus far, we have journeyed through our own internal landscape with Wati Kanyilpai, looking at ways to enhance and repair. It is time to extend our travel further. Come with Wati

Kanyilpai. Let us visit various organisations, political parties, the world of animals and plants, and our planetary ecosystems and see how we can promote nurturance in these larger domains.

The Family

Domestic violence is the core issue that we men must address in family life. It is one the chief sources of stress to young mothers and their babies' developing brains.

Toxic and hegemonic masculinity cultures and practices set the background, but if the male in the household also has a history of developmental trauma, domestic violence can become uncontrollable. The brain circuitry of a man with a history of developmental trauma is compromised in three key areas that impact on family life. The (1) **attachment** networks and programmes will make it difficult to develop good relationships, and when bonding *is* developed, any seeming threat to it will provoke (2) over-**intense emotional responses** because the right-brain amygdalar system is in a state of perennial hyper-arousal. And because (3) **impulse control** has also been compromised by DTD, the reaction can often degenerate into violence.

How to manage this? Becoming aware of one's developmental trauma is a good first step. One can then organise for some professional help.

Let me tell you the story of Bob, a young indigenous man living in one of the remote communities that I service because of attempted suicide. Bob had recently got married, but his wife was always criticising him and picking arguments. Bob was a 'good boy' who had taken in Community Health messages about the awful effects of domestic violence. He told me that when his wife tormented him so much that he wanted to kill her, he remembered that this was bad, and had so tried to kill himself instead.

I worked to develop as good a therapeutic alliance as possible with him. This was somewhat easier because I spoke his traditional language, Loritja.

I introduced him to the Wati Kanyilpai story and then said to him, in Loritja:

> *Wati Kanyilpai says to you, 'When your wife hurts you, say to her, "I feel hurt. I will leave the room for five minutes. When you come back, if she is still wrathful, then say, "I feel hurt again. I will go for a walk for fifteen minutes." If she still carries on, go to your brother's house for the afternoon. This can escalate to staying there overnight, then for a week, a month, even three months. If, after a three-month break she is still hurtful to you, this lets you know that she is unwilling/incapable of changing. Time for a divorce.'*

This fractionation approach moved his options beyond the two extreme ones (either I kill her, or I kill myself). Over the next few months, he and the rest of the family noticed a huge improvement in the wife's behaviour. She wasn't perfect, of course, but the relationship was much more manageable. And he was no longer suicidal.

Mental Health Organisations

Let us now go to the domain that I work in, psychiatry.

All the social workers, psychologists, psychiatrists, psychiatric nurses among you, this is especially for you.

I suspect that anything up to 95 per cent of the people we see/treat in various mental health services have early histories of developmental trauma or reactive attachment disorder. These histories in turn will have predisposed us to major psychiatric illnesses like schizophrenia and depression. But more broadly, they are the major factor behind a wide range of severe personality disorders like borderline, narcissistic, and dissociative conditions. But mainstream psychiatry seems to have a collective blind spot here. We tend to focus on treatment with antipsychotic and antidepression drugs but put much less emphasis on a secure and sustained therapeutic alliance, and lots of empathy and mindfulness work. Many organizations play 'Lego practitioner', with rapidly rotating personnel. This is a grotesquely mindless institutional denial of the importance of attachment dynamics. These institutions work in the mental health field and should know that if 95 per cent of their clientele have a DTD component to their problems, DTD always has an attachment dynamics element. And emotionally/relationally arid left-hemisphere-based methodologies like mainstream CBT are of limited use with these conditions.

As for the use of neurofeedback protocols that specifically address the chronically hypervigilant/hyper-aroused brain circuitry; even though all these are vital if our patients are to get some healing, there is not a single public or private sector psychiatric service in Australia that offers neurofeedback, with **the exception** of the STARTTS programme, the NSW Service for the Treatment and Rehabilitation of Torture and Trauma Survivors.

STARTTS is a specialist nonprofit organisation that, for thirty years, has provided culturally relevant psychological treatment and support, and community interventions, to help people and communities heal the scars of torture and refugee trauma and rebuild their lives in Australia. STARTTS also fosters a positive recovery environment through the provision of training to services, advocacy, and policy work. STARTTS began thirty years ago as a specialist team within a governmental area health service in Sydney to address a huge influx of traumatised refugees. It has since developed into a separately governed organisation with governmental and charity inputs and over one hundred full and part-time staff working from nine different offices and a range of outreach locations in metropolitan Sydney and in rural and regional areas (See http://www.startts.org.au/).

A service similar to this obviously needs to be extended to the general community, and a leading purpose of this book is to find ways of encouraging this.

In Chapter 4, we described the case of a young indigenous woman with a painful mental health history who had become pregnant. Child protection authorities were threatening to take the baby into care at birth. However, a fortuitous set of circumstances, including a very caring psychiatric nurse who was developing a good therapeutic alliance with her and the availability of a range of other supportive resources and personnel (including perinatal staff) working closely together made for a good outcome. The mother developed a good bond with her baby, who is now a thriving infant. This, in turn, gave the mother some vicarious repair. And there were positive flow-on effects to the rest of the family. If only cases like this were routine, rather than so exceptional that they warranted publication.

Schools

In my work with remote indigenous communities, I focus on the children as much as I can, despite protests from my administrators who think this takes away from work with adults. But the logic is simply that if we can intervene helpfully with kids in trouble, this may prevent trouble in adulthood.

This is where the schools become important. I have developed some strong collegial relationships with many of the teachers, who are keen to run empathy and mindfulness programmes with the children. I recently learned that one of the Papunya teachers had introduced a music programme for them. This of courses targets the right hemisphere, where so much of the damage lies. The results are so encouraging. The children become more interactive and caring. And in turn, their learning improves.

There has been a lot of work done in various parts of the world on this, identifying kids who have developmental trauma and bringing in programmes to address this.

There is a good overview by Geoff Lindsay (https://onlinelibrary.wiley.com/page/journal/14753588/homepage/school_interventions.htm 2018), who writes

> *There has been recent concern about the increasing number of children and adolescents with a wide range of mental health problems and the lack of appropriate provision to address the challenges related to this. Child guidance clinics/centres developed in the 1930s with teams consisting of a psychiatrist, educational or clinical psychologist and psychiatric social worker, but this clinic approach was found wanting primarily because it addressed such a small number of the young people who were in need of support. This led to the development*

of community-based educational psychology services many of which were based in schools (Desforges & Lindsay, 2018) and Child and Adolescent Mental Health Services (CAMHS). However, the increasing focus of schools recently on addressing the agenda of academic targets and the statutory requirements of local authorities to meet the special educational needs administrative requirements (most recently the Children & Families Act, 2014) have put great pressure on schools and educational psychologists, which has limited the opportunity for prevention and wider support.

Geoff reviews a range of English and European surveys on this topic.

These papers, collectively, provide an interesting and important body of studies on school-based interventions. Taken from different countries, with a range of methodologies and foci, the studies add to our knowledge of the prevalence of support for mental health and well-being interventions in schools and further, can provide some positive indications of what works and under what conditions. Importantly, they provide both positive and negative indications that will assist further research.

We need so much more of this.

If you're a teacher, do bring those nurturance skills into your work with the kids. It takes some time for a child to develop a secure attachment bond with you, but once that is in place, so many things become so much easier: attention, motivation, relational skills, constructive, and co-operative behaviours.

Child Care Agencies

This is a misery story riddled with poor assessments, abuse, neglect, and exploitation. Over the years, I've had many working connections with various governmental child care and protection organisations. Here is just one example.

I was looking after a woman who had bipolar illness and had a brief psychotic episode shortly after delivering a baby. The Child Protection Agencies took the baby away even though the woman had made a rapid recovery (days, not weeks). She was initially allowed access to her baby, and when I observed her interactions with the little one, I was confident that she would be able to develop a good bond with her and look after her properly. She was also getting a lot of support from me and my team. However, the Department of Child Services decided to discontinue the mother's access totally and send the baby off to a foster carer. We learned later that the designated carer was the sister of one of the child care workers and made a living out of looking after babies and children that had been taken away!

Even were these agencies to enhance their skills and services, there would still be the problem of availability. Today, in Australia, child protection systems continue to vary across states and territories. In most states, child protection services are part of a broader department of human services. Although a greater focus has been placed on prevention and providing family support services to families at risk of child abuse and neglect, statutory child protection services in each state and territory continue to struggle to meet demand (Holzer and Bromfield 2008).

Jarrod Wheatley was working as a social worker in Germany in 2011 when he experienced a light-bulb moment that led him to introduce a new out-of-home care model for vulnerable children in Australia—an accomplishment that saw the former Katoomba resident named 2019 NSW Young Australian of the Year last month.

> *'I witnessed a moment in Germany where this girl rested her head on her carer's shoulder at night-time when they were watching television,'* said Mr Wheatley.

The casual act of human connection went against everything he had been taught in Australia about professionals needing to keep distance from their clients.

> *'I'd been told in the work I'd done before that I had to keep a professional distance, and that's what it meant to be a professional. But here I was seeing a model in Germany that had counsellors, social workers, therapists, and psychologists all offering real relationships to children.'*

Or as the girl's carer told Mr Wheatley the next morning:

> *'Jarrod, it's not about professional distance. It's about professional nearness.'*

After further researching the model in his two-year stay in Germany, Mr Wheatley returned to Australia determined to introduce it here.

> *'Once you know there's a better way, it's pretty difficult to let the idea go,''* he said.

That determination would come in handy.

Getting the ground-breaking model—known as professional individualised care (PIC)—over Australia's bureaucratic hurdles took almost three years.

The first battle was gaining accreditation from the NSW Office of Children's Guardian, which only approved two types of children's care: foster care and group homes. The PIC model was neither.

It took Mr Wheatley a year to overcome this obstacle before he was able to work at gaining support from the department of Family and Community Services to fund the model.

Despite the slow process, the thirty-year-old said he never considered giving up.

> *'I think when you know the stakes are effectively children's lives—that sounds dramatic but that's how it feels for me—then the only appropriate response is to give it everything you've got,'* he said.

PIC places a child in the home of a professional therapeutic carer (PTC), who can develop a real relationship with the child. Prior to this, children who were too traumatised for a foster home would generally be placed in a group home where they were cared for by shift workers and were at risk of becoming institutionalised. In simple terms, it is individualised care rather than 'one size fits all'.

A registered charity in Australia, PIC was born from a partnership between Mountains Youth Service Team (MYST) and German organisation IJS, which has twenty-five years' experience operating the model in Germany.

IJS CEO Jürgen Reinfandt said part of the organisation's mission statement is 'to spread our idea all over the world'.

It provides a model of care for traumatised, neglected and abused children to give them a real chance to create their own life,

Mr Wheatley said the benefits of the PIC model cannot be overstated.

For a child who might have never lived in a home for more than three months, for them to be still living with someone a year later and regulating their emotions with an adult they trust, that's a huge step,

The heart of the model is real relationship. To achieve this you need committed, skilled Professional Therapeutic Carers. They are doing the most impressive work and they need to be paid as professionals.

Research has also shown the PIC model offers a better return on public funds in both the short and long term.

Australia still has a long way to go to catch up with Germany's embrace of the PIC model, where thirty-seven organisations provide care to more than 3,500 young people. PIC in Australia currently has eight careers looking after six young people.

'You get to what felt like the finish line at the start-up phase and you realise you're actually at the start of the race,' said Mr Wheatley.

But now the difficult groundwork has been carried out, other organisations and governments are likely to adopt the PIC model in Australia, changing children's lives as a result.

'Already in Australia I can see we've got children who maybe for the first time in their life have somewhere they belong and someone they can trust in,' said Mr Wheatley.

Do look up WHEATLEY on https://www.bluemountains gazette.com.au/ . . . /long-road-to-tra . . . /.

Toxic Masculinity, Hegemonic Patriarchy

In Chapter 2, we looked at how these deeply embedded cultural patterns exert powerful negative energies that affect women and children so badly. They contribute to domestic violence, maternal stress, and childhood trauma.

At which point, some things became clear. If we are to provide more adequate nurturance for our babies and infants, we must find effective ways of addressing toxic masculinity.

And we need to elaborate on Wati Kanyilpai's **benevolent** masculinity, one of the antidotes to toxicity. Hence the rest of this section.

Hegemonic Regimes and Religions

Grooming Children for Violence

The core thesis of this book is that those critical first few years of life have a huge input into how brain dynamics/brain programs that sustain mindfulness and empathy develop. And as we detailed earlier, mindfulness and empathy are two sides of the same relationships coin. Developmental trauma impairs both. Thus a damaged individual can be more easily stirred to murderous violence than a being who had good early nurturance.

And this can be taken advantage of by psychopathic elders, the aggressive equivalent of paedophilic groomers, who typically use religious tenets to incite vulnerable youngsters. They will first ensure that infants get a difficult start in life (which is inevitable in any highly sexist society), then ply the vulnerable infants with incitements to violence (encourage them use guns, sever the heads of enemies, etc.).

This in turn virtually guarantees that with every further generation the survivors will grow up to be psychopathic elders who will perpetuate the monstrous system.

Why do violent people use religion to justify their actions? One might naively imagine that a murderer would simply take pleasure in killing, without having to then invoke some religious principle to justify their action.

But this is not how it usually works. There is a sense in which all violence is predicated by pain. If I have had a problematic early developmental history, I will be relatively mindless, struggling to be aware of what is going on in myself, let alone anyone else. My emotional pain circuitry will be overactive. Thus I will be even more sensitive in certain ways than the average human being. I can be easily **shamed** and hurt (shame is a powerful facilitator of violence). I will also have poor impulse control. But staying with the awareness of this pain is much more difficult than just lashing out. So I lash out. Yet somewhere within me, there is a sense that this is not good. So I invoke a divine agency to justify it. I am doing it for Allah, Jehovah, or whatever.

As long as we humans have existed on this planet, we have been killing each other. The various religions that have developed during the Anthropocene have had mixed impacts on this slaughter. And since every religion places itself in an apical position in human society, it tends to receive apical praise and or blame *from* human society. But there are more fundamental factors at work. The current linkage of terrorism with Islamist offensives just does not get the point that murderousness actually prefigures religion. Even though Christianity, Judaism, Islam, Buddhism, Hinduism . . . have all been linked at various times with sanctioned killings, there are more fundamental factors at work, which then uses religion to justify itself. These factors are mindlessness and empathy failure, the consequences of poor early nurturance. Power-hungry humans, themselves the products of poor early nurturance, are often very good at using aspects of religion to stir up murderous impulses in their subordinates.

Let us look briefly at what the world's religions, the Jehovahs, the Allahs, the Brahmas, etc., have to say about child nurturance in those vital first two to four years of life.

Religions and Child Rearing Practices

Essentially, one can find nothing in **any** of the world religions on those aspects of child rearing that have to do with that vital preverbal dance of attunement during the first two or so years of life. I suppose one core factor is that the developmental neuroscience and attachment findings were not available at the time of their founding (the *developmental nurturance* megameme is, after all, a very recent development). Yet one imagines that a spiritual approach might carry a high level of intuition and empathy, and *something, somewhere* would have emerged about awarenesses of the special nature of those early years of life.

But this does not seem to be the case. There is quite a lot of ritualised prescription around circumcision, baptism, and the like and lots of recommendations for the rearing of somewhat older children, like 'Spare the rod and spoil the child', and introducing the child to various religious practices and beliefs, and so forth.

But there is very little on optimal infant/nurturer interactions. What is available falls more into the cultural/anthropological domain.

What religion were you brought up in? Do you have any religious affiliations now? How have your religious connections impacted on your understanding of infants in the first three years of life and how you might be with them?

Gardiner and Kosmitski, cross-cultural psychologists (Gardiner, H. W., and Kosmitzki, C. 2004) have written one of the very few books which looks at cross-cultural early child-rearing practices. In so far as religious beliefs are a major component of culture, their book at least gives us an indirect insight into whatever (few) intuitions some religions developed about early nurturance. Vicki Ritts, associate professor of Psychology and Behavioral Science at St. Louis Community College, also does a good review of Gardiner's *Lives Across Cultures: Cross-Cultural Human Development* (RITTS 2000), and again, religions just do not seem to bring much awareness to the subject.

The Politics of Attachment

Just as climate change is the biggest current threat to our earth's ecology, so is pervasive developmental trauma to our sociopsychological domain.

If we could only get those first three years of life right, a huge range of negative behavioural consequences would be reduced to more manageable levels: less violence, less terrorism, more empathy and compassion, more energy to apply to positive ends.

And yet there is not a single government on earth that has a well-developed policy on supportive interventions in the first three years of life. Not even the Scandinavian countries.

In the past few years, spurred on by increasing anxiety about child abuse, violent crime, delinquency, and drug misuse, public debate about the contribution of parents has become more intense. It has always been tempting to blame parents for the bad behaviour of their children, but there is a more thoughtful discussion. Without blame, it is possible to see what effects different kinds of parenting have on the lives of children, even extending into their own adult lives in the next generation. An enormous number of books and articles, conferences and policy statements have appeared, to the extent that we can say there is a movement towards supporting parents in their task. It is only possible to do this now that we understand just how difficult and stressful the task is. Until recently there was little public or professional acknowledgement of the immensity of parental commitment, perhaps because much of it was carried out by women, mostly mothers, whose voices were not heard. Even now it is easy for busy adults to resist a serious exploration of children's needs, because to do so arouses poignant memories of one's own childhood, both happy and sad, nostalgic and painful. In this chapter I outline a story of parenthood, from past to future, seen through the lens of attachment theory. Those working closely with families, such as health visitors, social workers, child carers and parent supporters in the voluntary sector need a coherent framework in which to understand family processes. They also need to know that their work cannot flourish in the absence of a coherent national policy on parenthood. The privatisation of children's care and needs is no longer an option. (Kramer and Roberts 1996)

Sebastian Kramer and colleagues (Kramer and Roberts 1996, Kramer in Dwivedi 1997) wrote well to this theme back in 1996, overviewing the field brilliantly, focusing on good attachment, consistency, sensitivity and responsiveness. But their observations were poorly received back then, and continue to be poorly received.

In the US earlier in 2018, nearly five hundred children of a group of Mexican immigrants were kept separated from their parents for months, as part of a new 'severity policy'. How did this come about? Presumably, the authors supposed that other potential immigrant mothers, motivated to come to America to gain better opportunities for their children, would decide not come if their children were to be harmed.

As a developmental neuropsychiatrist, I know that prolonged forced separation is as damaging to young children as physical or sexual abuse. How could civilized officials in a civilized country create such an abomination, reminiscent of Nazi outrages? Only if they were either emotional morons who were unaware of the damage this caused the children, or psychopaths who relished inflicting such harm.

And it was only when Donald Trump's wife Melania made a public plea for the children to be reunited with their carers that this sadistic policy began to recede.

And such immoral emotional mindlessness also occurred earlier in Australia, when in an attempt to deter 'people smugglers', a group of racketeers who charged huge fees for unsafe boat trips for undocumented asylum seekers trying to come to this country, various Australian governments set up 'off-shore processing' facilities. One of the most notorious is sited in Nauru, a Micronesian island over a thousand kilometres north east of Australia. What is especially troubling is that a large group of young children who had been detained there for over four years were enduring severe mental distress. A team from Médecins Sans Frontières were so alarmed that they made a strong protest to the government and the media and were deported as a consequence!

More recently, Dr Karen Phelps, newly elected Independent in the Australian parliament, made it one of her first tasks to propose a bill to immediately bring these children and their families to Australia and give them caring and support.

Wati Kanyilpai reminds us,

> *If a politician can demonstrate they genuinely care about children and nurturance (rather than acting out pretences and charades of caring), they deserve your support. Otherwise, if you can't trust them with kids, you can't trust them with anything.*

How to get the political parties in our nations involved in this vital task? They are **SO** not interested.

While I will be addressing how we can develop this in Australia, my country of origin, this is obviously more generally applicable.

As we said earlier, there is not a single nation or a single government on this planet that makes the issue of early nurturance its top priority to the extent of dedicating a *specific* public service department or ministry to it. What we need are ministers and ministries in early childhood nurturance, government agencies that can identify prospective mothers/fathers at risk and in stress, and deliver programmes that protect and nurture them, help them develop their nurturance skills, and ensure that the babies and infants can have a good enough early nurturance experience.

Nor for that matter is there a single political party anywhere that I am aware of that has made this issue a core priority in their election agendas. Politicians have short event horizons.

I also wonder if politics disproportionally attracts people with a certain amount of developmental trauma, persons who are driven to seek public glory to make up for early emotional neglect.

How can we encourage political parties to incorporate this in their agendas?

I suppose we could make a start by educating the public. It would be good to have a range of strong media presentations on the subject. In Australia, the public broadcaster Australian Broadcasting Corporation (ABC) could make a range of programmes for general consumption, examining findings in developmental neuroscience, looking at developmental trauma (the consequences of dysfunctional nurturance in those first three years) and featuring a range of preventive and reparative programmes like the Bumps to Babes and Beyond organisation we featured earlier.

The commercial media might then become interested in offering similar productions, and past a certain point, there would be sufficient public energy to impact on the political process.

Once this makes impacts sufficiently on the political system, some intensive thought and energy needs to be given to how to construct an early childhood nurturance programme.

An excellent role model would be the one offered by Bumps to Babes and Beyond, as detailed in Chapter 4, page 37.

The government of the day could also get lots of input from the Australian Childhood Foundation (detailed in Chapter 4).

The early nurturance ministry or public service agency would offer

1. early identification of mothers in stress/at risk;
2. lots of support, both social/emotional and practical (help with access to various government financial support systems, preparing layettes, etc.).
3. intensive training for the staff, to ensure their relational skills (sensitivity, empathy, mindfulness, and nurturance skills) were adequate.

The Financial Cost of Childhood Maltreatment

A final word for our politicians.

In 2012, Fang, Brown, Florence, et al. published a detailed analysis of the economic burden of child maltreatment in the United States and the economic implications for prevention.

The estimate of the aggregate lifetime cost of child maltreatment in 2008 was obtained by multiplying per-victim lifetime cost estimates by the estimated cases of new child maltreatment in 2008.

The findings were horrific. The total burden in the US was estimated to be as large as $585 billion!

Here is a direct quote from the authors' abstract.

Their Objectives:

To present new estimates of the average lifetime costs per child maltreatment victim and aggregate lifetime costs for all new child maltreatment cases incurred in 2008 using an incidence-based approach.

Their Methodology

This study used the best available secondary data to develop cost per case estimates. For each cost category, the paper used attributable costs whenever possible. For those categories that attributable cost data were not available, costs were estimated as the product of incremental effect of child maltreatment on a specific outcome multiplied by the estimated cost associated with that outcome. The estimate of the aggregate lifetime cost of child maltreatment in 2008 was obtained by multiplying per-victim lifetime cost estimates by the estimated cases of new child maltreatment in 2008.

Results:

The estimated average lifetime cost per victim of nonfatal child maltreatment is $210,012 in 2010 dollars, including $32,648 in childhood health care costs; $10,530 in adult medical costs; $144,360 in productivity losses; $7,728 in child welfare costs; $6,747 in criminal justice costs; and $7,999 in special education costs. The estimated average lifetime cost per death is $1,272,900, including $14,100 in medical costs and $1,258,800 in productivity losses. The total lifetime economic burden resulting from new cases of fatal and nonfatal child maltreatment in the United States in 2008 is approximately $124 billion. In sensitivity analysis, the total burden is estimated to be as large as $585 billion.

Conclusions:

> *Compared with other health problems, the burden of child maltreatment is substantial, indicating the importance of prevention efforts to address the high prevalence of child maltreatment.* (Fang et al 2012)

The event horizon for remedy is a long one and, hence, unlikely to appeal to politicians of any persuasion, but if enough public awareness and pressure can be brought to this fundamental issue, it may just encourage our leaders to begin to take some active remedial steps. Wati Kanyilpai appeals to all of us to do what we can to create more public awareness.

Finale

Let us give Wati Kanyilpai the final words.

> *Wai, walytja tjuta. Dear fellow beings. How can we help our poor struggling world? The one single thing we can do is to expand our nurturance skills (kanyintja). As more empathy and mindfulness and loving-kindness arises, the awful ravenousness, violence, abuse, and exploitation that plagues our world dwindles (kura tjuta wyiaringanyi).*
>
> *Parenting is a core task in this nurturance project. It has not changed much over the millennia, but it is only in the past few decades, with the help of greater understanding emerging from advances in the developmental neuroscience, that we have been able to spell out clearly what it involves. Even thousands of years ago, you might find children and parents doing similar things to what they do now. Babies are the same now as they were then and so are their needs. The first*

thing a baby needs is to be held and interacted with, and most of us instinctively feel this, even with other people's babies. We are programmed to be interested in tiny children, and are all familiar with the way in which babies in prams can hypnotise us with their big eyes. Even hyperactive teenagers are calmed for a moment by the experience.

The higher primates of today, the chimpanzees and gorillas, probably represent something like our prehuman ancestors, and they look after their offspring in quite familiar ways. The popularity of zoos and nature programmes on TV has a lot to do with the fact that we can identify so readily with animals, particularly those that form attachments between adults and infants.

Newborn humans are particularly fragile because they still have a lot of developing to do. They are nowhere near ready for any kind of independence. None of this is new. It has been like that for tens of thousands of years.

This nurturance needs to be extended to ourselves, our families, our social groups, our various organizations, and the political system.

Please do whatever you can to support nurturance, look after those young mothers and babies (nguntjunya munu pipirinya palya kanyini), and ensure a good future for our planet (ngura tjuta).

Palya nyinanyi, pukulpa nyinanyi, pylunpa nyinanyi walytja tjuta. Walytja tjutanya

Atunymananyi, kaWati Kanyilpai Tjukurpa nyuranya tjuta atunymankuku.

Be well, be happy, be peaceful. Look after everybody, and Wati Kanyilpai's Nurturance Dreaming will protect you all.

BIBLIOGRAPHY

Bromfield, L., Richardson, N., and Holzer, P. (2008). Australian Institute of Family Studies. National Child Protection. Clearinghouse National Commonwealth of Australia *2008*.

Fang, X., Brown, D. S., Florence, C. S., Mercy, J. A. (2012). 'The Economic Burden of Child Maltreatment in the United States and Implications for Prevention'. *Child Abuse Negl.* Feb; 36 (2):156-65. doi: 10.1016/j.chiabu.2011.10.006. Epub 2012 Feb 1.

Fisher, S. F. (2014). *Neurofeedback in the Treatment of Developmental Trauma: Calming the Fear-Driven Brain.* New York, NY, US: W W Norton & Co.

Gardiner, H., Komitski, C. (2008). *Lives Across Cultures, 4th Edition.* ISBN-13: 9780205494750.

Grewen, K. M., Girdler, S. S., Amico, J., and Light, K. C. (2005). 'Effects of Partner Support on Resting Oxytocin, Cortisol, Norepinephrine, and Blood Pressure Before and After Warm Partner Contact'. *Psychosomatic Medicine.* Jul–Aug; 67(4):531–8.

Felitti, V. J., Anda, R. F., et al. (1998) 'Relationship of Childhood Abuse and Household Dysfunction to Many of the Leading Causes of Death in Adults: The Adverse Childhood Experiences (ACE) Study'. *American Journal of Preventive Medicine.* Vol. 14. May.

Hewlett, B. S., Lamb, M. E. (2005). *Hunter-Gatherer Childhoods: Evolutionary, Developmental, and Cultural Experiences.* New Brunswick, NJ. Aldine. (See esp. p. 15).

Jarrett, C. (2016), on *Research Digest* at https://digest.bps.org.uk/2016/11/28/the-psychology-of-eye-contact-digested/.

Kraemer, S., and Roberts, J. (eds.) (1996). *Towards a Secure Society*. London: Free Association Books, 1996

Kraemer, S. (1997). 'Parenting Yesterday Today and Tomorrow'. Chapter in *Enhancing Parenting Skills* ed K. N. DWIVEDI. John Wiley & Sons, Chichester. 1997.

Lindsay, G. (2018). 'Child and Adolescent Mental Health' online. https://onlinelibrary.wiley.com/page/journal/14753588/homepage/school_interventions.htm.

Leong, V., et al. (2017). 'Speaker Gaze Increases Infant-Adult Connectivity'. *PNAS*; 28 Nov; DOI: 10.1101/108878.

Linden, D. (2015). *Touch: The Science of Hand, Heart and Mind*. Viking Press 2015.

Meares, R. (2012). *Borderline Personality Disorder and the Conversational Model: A Clinician's Manual*. NORTIN. October. ISBN 978-0-393-70783-0.

Narvaez, D., Panksepp, J., Schore, A., and Gleason, T. R. (2013). 'Evolution, Early Experience and Human Development' from *Research to Practice and Policy*. Oxford University Press.

Nowak, M. A., Highfield, R., (2011). *Supercooperators: Altruism, Evolution, and Why We Need Each Other to Succeed*. Free Press. ISBN-13: 978-1451626636

ISBN-10: 1451626630.

Petchkovsky, L., San Roque, C., (2002). '*Tjunguwyiantja,* Attacks on Linking: Forced Separation and its Psychiatric Sequelae in Australia's "Stolen Generations"'. *J Transcultural Psychiatry,* Sept. Vol 39 (3) 345–366.

Ritts, V. (2000). Book Review: *Lives Across Cultures: Cross-Cultural Human Development.* Harry W. Gardiner, Jay D. Mutter, and Corinne Kosmitzki. BOSTON, MA: ALLYN and BACON, (1998), 330 pp. *International Journal of Group Tensions* 29(3):386–388 December 2000 DOI: 10.1023/A:1026537715431.

Robertson-Gillam, K., Petchovsky, L. (2015). 'Choir Singing as a Psychotherapeutic Intervention for Reducing Depression in Mid to Older Age: A Controlled Trial with QEEG Testing'. May 2015. *J Music Therapy.*

Siegel, D. (2012). 'Mindfulness and Empathy Practices'. http://www.drdansiegel.com/resources/wheel_of_awareness/.

STARTTS. http://www.startts.org.au/

Watson, J. B. (1928). *Psychological Care of Infant and Child.* New York: W.W. Norton Company, Inc.

Wheatley, J. on https://www.bluemountainsgazette.com.au/ . . . /long-road-to-tra . . . /

Weinhold, B. and J. (2015). 'The Politics of Developmental Trauma'. http://weinholds.org/the-politics-of-developmental-trauma/. April.

Wylie, M. S. (2010). 'The Long Shadow of Trauma' (2010). *Psychotherapy Networker,* April. *www.psychotherapynetworker.org.*

INDEX

Indigenous People   x, 93, 95

J

Johnson, William   109-10

K

kanyintja   9, 20, 94, 184
kensho   19, 29

L

Lecter, Hannibal   77, 147
left hemisphere   55, 71-3, 152
Louise (Agnes's daughter)   19
loving-kindness   102, 144-5, 147-8, 150, 162, 184

M

Machiavellianism   38-9
Maine, Mary   49
Medicine Snake   2-3
Medicine Snake Dreaming   2
meditation   14-15, 80, 102, 146-9
megamemes   27, 30-5, 42
meme   30, 33, 81
Men   ix-1, 4, 7-10, 18, 20, 23-5, 28, 36-42, 67, 97, 102-3, 123-5, 143-4, 163-4
mindfulness   1, 7-8, 11-15, 20-2, 24-5, 29, 37, 46, 60, 64, 74, 79-81, 98-9, 101-2, 105, 107, 109, 115, 129-31, 145-7, 153-4, 162-3, 166, 168, 174, 182, 184
mirroring   75
MOS Plus   129
mothers   3, 6, 16-17, 19, 27, 32-3, 36, 41, 49-50, 58, 60, 62, 64, 66-71, 74-5, 80-1, 94, 97-101, 103, 114, 116, 119, 122-4, 128, 130-1, 133, 143, 146, 156-7, 161-2, 164, 167, 178-9, 182, 185

music   110, 132, 151

N

narcissism   11, 38, 77
near enemies   147
neurofeedback   107, 111, 132, 162, 166
ngangkari   ix, 2-3, 94
nurturance   ix, 1, 3-4, 7-10, 13, 15-25, 28-9, 32-7, 42, 45-7, 54, 57-8, 60-1, 63-5, 69, 71, 73-4, 76-81, 95, 97-104, 110, 115, 117-25, 127, 130, 142-3, 163-4, 169, 174, 176-7, 180-2, 184-6
nurturance failure   ix, 15, 58, 63, 76, 80
'nurture the nurturers'   ix, 3, 5, 8, 12, 14, 16-17, 20, 23-4, 36, 71, 81, 99-100, 113, 119, 122, 124-5, 128, 130, 151, 163

P

perspectival empathy   77-8, 147
professional individualised care (PIC)   172-3
programmes of repair   132-3
psychodrama   74-5
psychopathy   11, 29, 38, 60, 79
psychotherapy   7, 14-15, 60, 69, 74, 80, 98, 102, 107, 115, 132-3, 145-6, 150, 161-2

Q

QEEG (quantitative EEG)   15, 61-2, 111, 151
quantitative EEG   62, 111

R

rats   92
reactive attachment disorder (RAD)   57, 60, 80, 106-8, 112, 166

Printed in Australia
AUHW010515071020
335143AU00001B/4